'An amazingly inspiring book coming at just the right moment. A leading light in an invaluable organisation, Matthew Bolton really knows how to make stuff happen – and he wants you to know too. You might have heard that things don't have to be this way – here's the official guidebook to changing them' Marina Hyde, *Guardian*

'I want to congratulate you on the brilliant way, and the ruthless way, that you bend us politicians to your will, and you get us to deliver' Boris Johnson, then Mayor of London, to Citizens UK

'Matthew is one of the great thought and action leaders of his generation. This book will give people the power to change their communities' Tessa Jowell

'Populism is the most important political development of our time, and *How to Resist* makes a powerful call for a populism of mass democratic participation. We've got to put power back in people's hands and this vital guide tells us how. It's a must-read' Steve Hilton, co-founder and CEO of political action website Crowdpac and bestselling author of *More Human*

'There's a huge appetite right now for radical change, and *How to Resist* can equip a generation of politically engaged young people with the practical tools to organise and campaign' Paul Mason, bestselling author of *Postcapitalism*

'With expertise and a track record that is compelling, Matthew offers tools for citizens to become more powerful and stand up to the vested interests of the market and state. This book offers a vision and a method to revitalise our democracy' Philip Blond, Director of Res Publica, author of *Red Tory*

'If anyone knows how to do social change, it's Matthew Bolton, who has been at the heart of Citizens UK's successful Living Wage campaign. He's a smart, sophisticated operator and his book imparting nuggets on how to take on the system will be eagerly pored over by people who are keen to make a difference but don't quite know how to go about it' David Cohen, Campaigns Editor and Chief Feature Writer, *London Evening Standard*

'The Living Wage is perhaps the most successful grassroots campaign of the last decade and in *How to Resist*, Matthew gives us the key lessons and tactics behind the impact. This vital book will help turn the political energy of today into lasting change in communities and constituencies up and down the country' Polly Toynbee, *Guardian*

'I talk about the Big Society; you are the Big Society' David Cameron, then Leader of the Conservative Party, to Citizens UK

HOW TO RESIST

HOW TO RESIST

Turn Protest to Power

MATTHEW BOLTON

BLOOMSBURY

LONDON · OXFORD · NEW YORK · NEW DELHI · SYDNEY

Bloomsbury Publishing
An imprint of Bloomsbury Publishing Plc

50 Bedford Square   1385 Broadway
London   New York
WC1B 3DP   NY 10018
UK   USA

www.bloomsbury.com

BLOOMSBURY and the Diana logo are trademarks of Bloomsbury Publishing Plc

First published in Great Britain 2017

British Library Cataloguing-in-Publication Data
A catalogue record for this book is available from the British Library.

Library of Congress Cataloguing-in-Publication data has been applied for.

ISBN: HB: 978-1-4088-9272-5
         EPUB: 978-1-4088-9273-2

2 4 6 8 10 9 7 5 3 1

Typeset by Integra Software Services Pvt. Ltd.
Printed and bound in Great Britain by CPI Group (UK) Ltd, Croydon CR0 4YY

To find out more about our authors and books visit www.bloomsbury.com. Here you
will find extracts, author interviews, details of forthcoming events and the option to sign
up for our newsletters.

For Frances and Ray

Contents

Introduction   1

1   If You Want Change, You Need Power   25

2   Appreciating Self-Interest   37

3   Practical Tools to Build Power   51

4   Turning Problems into Issues   61

5   The Action is in the Reaction   77

6   Practical Tools to Build a Campaign   99

7   Unusual Allies and Creative Tactics   115

8   Finding the Time   131

9   The Iron Rule   139

Acknowledgements   157

Introduction

This book is for people who are angry with the way things are and want to do something about it; for people who are frustrated with the system, or worried about the direction the country is going in. For people who are upset about a particular issue, or want a greater say in the changes happening in their neighbourhood. They've posted their opinions on social media and they've shouted at something they've seen on the news. They've been on the big march and they've been to the ballot box, but what more can be done? This is for people who want to make a change, but they're not sure how.

This book isn't going to tell you what you ought to care about, or make the case for any particular policy or politician. I have my values and they will show, but this book is about how you can make a difference to the things that you believe in. It offers a tried-and-tested method and a set of practical tools and principles to show how people can get together and make change happen. It's not about how the political system works and how other people govern on our behalf. It's about how people themselves can challenge the system and influence decision-making whichever politicians are in power.

There is a moment of opportunity right now. January 2017 saw 100,000 take part in the Women's March in London as part of a worldwide demonstration of solidarity totalling 21 million people. Under the banner of resistance, we've seen a rise in protests and mobilisations on both sides of the Atlantic. The June 2017 UK general election saw turnout amongst 18–25 year olds surge to an estimated 66% and for the third time in a year, following Brexit and Trump, an election result that saw unexpectedly high numbers reject the status quo and defy the expectations of the elite. These are powerful and profound shifts in political engagement, and it's clear there is real anger and appetite for change. But we need to channel this anger into ongoing democratic participation – beyond the single act of voting or the occasional protest. We need a generation of activists and organisers campaigning for change. All politics is ultimately local, and we have an opportunity to create thousands of active citizens making change in their communities and lobbying MPs in constituencies. This energy can help create a better society, but it's also critical that we channel the anger into something constructive and collaborative, because anger without power tends to lead to rage.

The question is: how do we resist? The motivation behind protest is usually good, but too often the method is missing.

Even in the word 'resist' there's a danger of starting off on the back foot, of handing over the initiative to others: someone else has the plan and we are just reacting to it. It can feel like the resistance is just a series of one-off symbolic protests aimed at raising awareness but lacking specific aims or a strategy to achieve them. We may feel momentarily powerful gathering in large numbers but, if we're honest, it's too often a disparate coalition brought together around a host of different causes or abstract principles. If this is the way we resist then, as quickly as this energy for activism has, it will pass in disappointment, and the opportunity will be lost.

This book shows how to turn that symbolic protest into a strategy for power and change. It's about how people can come together to make their own plan and work together to achieve it. I inherited and have now practised for twelve years a method that can be learnt and used by anyone who wants to make a difference. It doesn't require some special position or qualification and it doesn't require loads of money or an impossible amount of spare time. It's as old as politics itself and it's about how those without much power can come together and change things.

It all begins with what makes you angry, what you care about deeply enough to act on. It requires a radical rethink of the way we understand power and self-interest, and places those two concepts at the heart of an argument about how politics and change really work. It offers a method and tactics for how people can take on those with financial power and authority, and win.

The starting point is: if you want change, you need power. You build up power through relationships with other people around common interests. You break down the big problems you face together into specific issues and identify who the decision-makers are, who has the power to make the changes you need. Then you take action to get a reaction and build a relationship with the decision-makers. If they don't agree to implement the changes then you escalate the action or turn to more creative tactics, learning as you go and celebrating the small wins as you build incrementally up to the bigger issues. To complement this strategy there is a set of skills and tools that together make up an approach called 'community organising'.

What's at stake here is more important than simply helping people who care about particular issues to run effective campaigns. It's about democracy. In the past, people who wanted to make a difference and believed in change fought for democracy with sweat, blood and courage. The Chartists, the Suffragettes and others endured prison and faced death in their struggle for the chance to have a say in the governance of the country. They organised and campaigned to force the ruling elites to open up our political system to influence by the majority of the people. It is a great misunderstanding to think that they were fighting for the chance to put a cross in a box once every few years. They were fighting – week in, week out – for power. Fighting for more people to have more influence.

Over time, we have become confused. Now we have the vote, we have mistaken politics for Parliament and have come to see democracy as something to watch on television or follow on Twitter, like spectators at a football game – or worse, to switch off from it completely, losing trust in politicians, losing trust in the media, losing trust in the system. Democracy doesn't just mean 'to vote', it means people power. It means embedding political action into our day-to-day lives, in our communities and workplaces. It is a vision of a society where power is distributed amongst the people, not concentrated in the hands of the few. It's not an end state, but a constant struggle for people to fight for a seat around the decision-making table.

But it doesn't feel like we are at the table. It feels like we are on the menu. Power is being concentrated in the hands of an increasingly small circle of people. We have a revolving door of Cabinet ministers becoming bankers, becoming newspaper editors, becoming chief executives. We have been lulled into a false sense of security, thinking that our democratic system would create a better future for us all. But it doesn't look that way. By lunchtime on the first Wednesday in January, after just two-and-a-half days' work, FTSE 100 bosses will have earned more than the average person will earn that entire year. The generation now in their twenties will be the first in modern times to be worse off than their parents. What we want for ourselves and our children – a decent job, a home, a health service, a community – is under threat.

People are waking up, getting angry and looking for ways to fight back. Last year, 2016, saw two huge shocks to the Western political system – Brexit and Trump. Wildly different, they had one thing in common: both political campaigns tapped straight into popular discontent, a feeling that the people were being ignored. Into this feeling of distrust and powerlessness came the most potent phrase in the last thirty years of UK politics: 'Take back control.' Why was that so powerful? Because it captured a mood. People do feel like they have lost control – not just of what happens in Parliament, but of what happens in their neighbourhoods, and what will become of their lives. But guess what? Article 50 of the Treaty of Lisbon has been triggered and over two-thirds of people still feel like they have little or no control over Westminster politics, local government or what happens in their neighbourhoods. A once-in-a-lifetime referendum vote, with all the actual implications for our futures, worked out by a small team of politicians, is not people taking back control.

Whatever you think about the advantages and disadvantages of the European Union, there is no denying that, while formally democratic, it had become utterly distant from the lives of people across the UK. Most of us couldn't name our MEP or describe what the EU really did. How can we be surprised that people withdrew their consent? But, if we are honest, that is how many people feel about their MPs and local councillors. That's how they feel about Westminster. Trust in politicians is decreasing and a gap is opening up between those who govern and those they serve. When people lose trust in the political system it's a dangerous time. It leaves people vulnerable to manipulation, to being offered someone to blame, to one group being pitted against another.

From some commentators we hear warnings of the dangers of populism. 'We can't trust the people. They will tear each other apart, or tear the system down. They don't know what's best for them...' So what is the answer? Take power further away from people? It's not the people we must fear but the increasing spread of disenfranchisement and distrust. The worst thing that can happen now is for democrats to cede the idea of a popular politics to demagogues who stir up prejudice and set one group against another. What we are seeing is a populism of division, where a small number of powerful people have tuned their political messages and their voter analytics to tap into feelings of distrust and disengagement and offer someone easy to blame, whether it's immigrants, foreign powers or an unspecified evil 'elite'.

We need to reclaim populism. The *Oxford English Dictionary* defines it as 'support for the concerns of ordinary people'. We need more of that, not less. This book calls for a new populism: the mass participation of people in politics in pursuit of their interests. Not populism as an approach by politicians to divide and rule, but populism as democracy, for the people by the people. This will benefit those who currently get a raw deal, as they organise together for better jobs and housing and to have more influence on the decisions affecting them and their communities. And it will benefit us all, because it is through political participation that we will maintain the legitimacy of our democratic institutions and keep the peace. As the agents of change, however big or small, we are forced to find allies and so learn that our interests are bound up with others who are different from us. Through trying to actually get things done, we realise that those with authority are human beings, to be worked with, to be held to account and, as often as not, to be trusted. We need a populism of mass participation so that people, who for decades have felt that change is always something that is being done to them, get a taste of power and realise they can be the ones making the change.

How will we get there? Some policy changes can be made by government, to create platforms for 'citizen engagement' and drive towards devolution and transparency. Some of these changes are happening: this kind of thinking has been gaining ground over the last two decades in UK political thought, on the left and right. But it's a mistake to think that this problem will be solved by politicians. In his idea of the 'big society', Prime Minister David Cameron saw community organising as a promising way to increase social action. When I took him around the Ocean Estate in Mile End, on the morning that he launched his 'big society' vision in April 2010, I said to him that the fundamental aim of community organising was for people to build and use power, to have control over decision-making and to hold the state and market to account. But that core purpose of changing the power dynamics was conspicuously absent from the various initiatives that ultimately came out of the 'big society'. The government-funded community organising programme got people listening, but it didn't build the kind of people power needed to tackle underlying injustice or create policy change. The building of people's capacity to hold politicians to account is unlikely to be done on a Cabinet Office grant.

The then Leader of the Opposition, Ed Miliband, looked to community organising for how it might help the Labour Party operate more like a grassroots movement. He said he wanted the party to 'be more like Citizens UK' and he employed the services of a community organiser from the United States to make it more focused on building relationships, and more member-led. Alongside this attempt to shift the internal culture,

Ed Miliband oversaw radical changes to the Labour leadership election rules to a 'one member, one vote' system that thrust Jeremy Corbyn into leadership and held him there against the judgement of the majority of Labour MPs. By putting power in the hands of people, this shift created a counter-cultural political force that proved to be significantly more in tune with the electorate than people thought. In the third political shock of the last twelve months, Corbyn's case for change proved to be nearly as popular as Theresa May's case for stability. The hung parliament that we now have, for as long as it lasts, means greater opportunity for us to influence decision-making. Every MP's vote counts in the House and every MP, especially those in tight seats and with the prospect of another general election soon, will listen to their constituents if they organise and campaign effectively. Now is not the time for people to disengage from political activity. On the contrary, the challenges we are facing as a society are too much for politicians to shoulder on their own, especially with Westminster in such a precarious position. We can't wait for the next election; we must take action for what we believe in now.

There is plenty more that could be said on the rapidly shifting political terrain, but this book is not about policy, political parties and Parliament. With all due respect to those who serve our society as elected politicians, there are more than enough books and column inches dedicated to the activities and intrigues of Westminster. This book is about the role of the people. How can we be effective citizens? Of all the problems we face, surely the invigoration of our political culture is one that we must help tackle ourselves, rather than expect politicians to solve for us.

Ultimately the health of a democracy rests in the abilities and attitudes of the people towards their own role in governance. Yes, it's in the balance of powers between the Cabinet, the House of Commons and House of Lords, and in the independence of the judiciary and media. But the accountability and legitimacy of these institutions relies on the participation and engagement of the people. What preoccupies me most is the question of where the great majority of people will learn the tools of democratic participation, and how they will come to know that their voice matters. We are all updated minute-by-minute on the twists and turns of an increasingly frenetic political news cycle, but we are left feeling less able to influence the decisions affecting us. That is the reason I am writing this book: to offer a method for people to channel their concerns into making change. My experience of building a movement of citizens over the last twelve years is that it's in collective action and in local associations that people learn to lead, to listen, to cooperate and to compromise, the fundamental skills and attitudes that underpin a democratic society.

In times past, the churches played perhaps the most significant role. If we think of some of the great institutions we benefit from today – hospitals, schools, housing associations, trade unions and charities – these were often developed in, or sponsored by, local churches. As the primary gathering place of a local community, connecting with each other around a tradition of hope and service, the churches gave birth to many of the great social innovations and also many of the great social justice campaigns, such as the abolition of slavery. While it may be awkward for many who are secular, we still desperately need faith communities to play this role. But we need other institutions too. Schools, hospitals and workplaces – places where people come together regularly with a positive purpose – have great potential to be the engines of democratic participation over the coming decades. However, it requires a reinvention of their role and a broadening of their responsibilities and repertoires. Rather than getting stuck on the narrower focus – of treating people once they're sick, of producing SATs and GCSE results, on the short-term shareholder return – they need instead to adopt a focus on new civic responsibility, of teaching and enabling democratic skills, developing new responses to social problems, and fomenting conversations and conspiracies for positive political change.

It is in the invigoration of existing civic institutions and the creation of new ones that we can find the greatest hope for a society, not of subjects or consumers, but of citizens. The next stage of our emancipation can be achieved through the education of the people in effective political participation. But we are at a crossroads. If we don't equip the people with the skills to make change, and if we don't trust them to have power, then they will be resigned to apathy, will continue to lose trust in those who govern on their behalf and be open to manipulation and division by those who seek to gain power through exploiting discontent. Anger must be channelled into democratic action. Politics is indeed too important to be left to the politicians. So vote, always vote, but that's the bare minimum. Your democracy needs you. Yes, you.

When we think about the big challenges facing us over the coming decades, what can one person do? It's a struggle enough just to get the kids to school, to pay the bills, to get through a week at work, to remember to fill out that form and send it off in time. To survive the hangover and the busy commute. The trials and tribulations of life are common to us all. But all the individuals in all the great stories of social change through history are normal people just like you and me. This book is about how they did it. So let's consider two such people, two moments of social change, and two unexpected things they had in common.

The story of Rosa Parks you probably know: the African American woman who famously refused to give up her seat on a bus when the driver asked a row of black passengers to move for a white man. Her arrest in 1955 gave rise to huge public outcry and started the Montgomery bus boycott. The boycott of public buses lasted 381 days and around three-quarters of the bus company's passengers opted to walk instead. The young Baptist minister Martin Luther King Jr was appointed to lead the Montgomery Improvement Association, and help organise the boycott. After just over a year, the US Supreme Court ruled that segregation on buses was unconstitutional. It was a huge victory and a turning point in the American civil rights movement. One brave woman setting in motion a campaign that changed the course of history.

The story of Abdul Durrant you probably don't know: the black British Muslim man who worked nights as a cleaner at HSBC's headquarters in Canary Wharf – that futuristic centre of global capital, full of skyscrapers and jewellery shops. Abdul was one of thousands of workers on the minimum wage in insecure employment. Every night he cleaned the offices of Sir John Bond, who earned £2 million a year as chairman of the bank. At the annual general meeting of the bank in 2003, Abdul came not as a cleaner but as a shareholder, having connected with others to buy shares and legitimate access to the company's annual moment of public accountability. He stood up in front of all the investors and executives, nervous as anything, and said: 'Sir John, we work in the same office but we live in different worlds. Let me tell you what it's like to work on £4.50 per hour and bring up six children.' This David and Goliath confrontation hit the headlines and within eighteen months, HSBC and also neighbouring Barclays had increased the pay of its cleaners. It was a turning point in the UK Living Wage campaign, which has lifted hundreds of thousands of people out of working poverty and changed the government's approach to the minimum wage.

And the two unexpected things in common? First, as an interesting aside, the march that Martin Luther King Jr was on when he was shot dead in Tennessee in 1968 – after he had become perhaps the most famous civil rights leader in the world – was a protest for a Living Wage for cleaners. The very same issue Abdul

Durrant fought for on a different continent almost forty years later. Second, Rosa Parks and Abdul Durrant were both trained in campaigning. Both were leaders in social change organisations. Their actions were not spontaneous acts of individual courage. They were key moments, planned and orchestrated as part of ongoing strategies by a group of people who came together in order to effect change. Such stories tend to be told in terms of a lone hero or heroine who changes the course of history. While this may be inspirational, it is so singular and superhuman as to become almost inimitable. How could they just suddenly do something like that? The reality is something quite different. There are strategies and methods we can take from these stories and put into practice in our own lives.

Rosa Parks had been active in the civil rights struggle for ten years before the bus action. She was secretary of the Montgomery chapter of the National Association for the Advancement of Colored People (NAACP). She had been trained at the Highlander Folk School, a centre for Civil Rights activists. The Montgomery NAACP had been planning a bus boycott for at least a year and had been looking for the right person to be a test case to take to the courts. There had already been at least three other black passengers that year who had refused to give up their seats, but in those cases there weren't the right ingredients for the strategy to catch light. With Rosa, however, it did.

In 2003, Abdul Durrant was a leader in the East London Communities Organisation, part of Citizens UK. He had been trained in leadership and public action by the Citizens UK community organising programme. Community organisers had been in and around Canary Wharf for two years, meeting with cleaning staff and testing out potential leaders and possible actions. On that day at the bank's AGM, Abdul was part of a team of people that included east London clergy, community organisers and others. The media were tipped off in advance so they could cover the action. It was all part of a campaign involving thousands of people and many other actions at HSBC branches and outside the company's headquarters that led to the breakthrough. These less well-known parts of the stories are important: the teams, the training, the planning, the failed attempts. It all starts to make a bit more sense. You realise that Rosa and Abdul weren't superhuman. Rosa and Abdul were trained and were part of organisations operating according to a method and a strategy. They were just two people who played a particularly prominent role alongside others. It makes you think: what role could I play? What organisation should I be part of and what method do I need to use?

When in the future people look back at the great moments of social change in the twenty-first century, who will they talk about? It could be you. And there are hundreds of thousands of people out there who want things to change. But the question remains: how can we channel this energy and potential into something that makes a real and positive difference?

I recall the financial crisis of 2008 and the widespread anger, fear and soul-searching that was experienced as people considered what this would mean for our economic future and system. It was a moment when people power for change was really needed, a moment for a political response driven by the concerns of ordinary people. So initial hopes were high when the Occupy London movement was launched with its radical call to change capitalism. The protest dominated the news and front pages for days on end. Maybe this was the beginning of some real change?

But what happened? The protestors wanted an end to inequality, a reverse of the cuts in government spending and an overhaul of the global economic system. The protest had first intended to camp outside the London Stock Exchange but was blocked by an injunction, so ended up at St Paul's Cathedral, where the protesters occupied the square. Over three months in 2011–12, the protest turned into an increasingly ramshackle camp of tents outside St Paul's, and the most specific impacts of the protest ended up being the resignation of several Anglican clergy, rather than any changes to the financial system. The right motives and the right moment, but without method and strategy you don't get very far when you're up against the excesses of global capitalism. Ultimately it puts people off – because it looks as though protest doesn't work.

My mind goes back further, to the anti-war protests of February 2003 – the first march that I went on – when close to a million people gathered in opposition to the proposed invasion of Iraq. It was the largest public protest in British history and part of a wave of demonstrations in 600 cities across the world. But the invasion still went ahead the following year; the war turned out to be a disaster and the claims of weapons of mass destruction exaggerated. The people called it right but the politicians carried on regardless, with terrible consequences. Such huge public opposition at the time added to the later sense that people had been lied to and that their political representatives weren't to be trusted. It likely raised the bar even higher for any politician thinking about future intervention – in Syria, for example. So there were some effects, but the experience of the great majority of people on the march was that the protest didn't achieve its aim. I know I was left thinking: it was a good thing to do, but it didn't work. What more could I have done? And you've probably been party to a conversation that goes something like this:

YOUR MATE: 'How was the march?'

YOU: 'Yeah it was good. There were lots of people and it didn't rain.'

YOUR MATE: 'Cool. What do you think will happen as a result?'

YOU: 'Dunno, but I'm glad I went.'

Well, this book is about what you do beyond the march. When you get home – day to day, week on week. It's about how you can focus on something specific that you care about, work with others to make a tangible difference, and build up from making small changes to making bigger ones. It is the tried and tested method of 'community organising'.

Barack Obama was a community organiser before training as a lawyer and later becoming president. He now talks about returning to – or at least devoting energy to supporting – community organising. The method originated partly out of frustration that the US civil rights movement dissipated once it achieved its incredible successes in legislative change. Community organising was pioneered by the American Saul Alinsky and then further established through the work of Citizens UK's sister organisation in the US, the Industrial Areas Foundation. Citizens UK has adopted and amended it for the British context over the last twenty-five years. It aims to build permanent people-power organisations that can train citizens, strengthen communities and achieve incremental change.

Of all the various approaches to making change, I'm focusing on community organising for three reasons. First, it's what I know. Second, it's accessible to every-one, including those who start with very little power: it doesn't require large sums of money, status, or highly technical skills, it just requires the appetite to work together with others for change. Thirdly, it works. I have spent over a decade doing it and I have seen ordi-nary people do extraordinary things using these tools. I have worked together with thousands of others to help build the UK Living Wage campaign, which has won hundreds of millions of pounds in pay increases for over 150,000 low-paid workers. The campaign has persuaded thousands of employers to go beyond the legal minimum and pay people what it really costs to live; it has inspired Living Wage movements across the world, and has created a new political consensus here in the UK. When the Conservative government introduced the 'National Living Wage' in 2015, while effectively a higher minimum wage and not a full Living Wage, it meant that the force of what began as a local grassroots campaign has now brought higher wages to millions of low-paid workers. Alongside the big campaigns there have been countless smaller impacts on neighbourhood issues, the bread and butter of community organising. And of course there have been mistakes, wasted efforts and laughable failures, and I will include some of those in what follows, alongside the successes.

And it all starts with the question: What makes you angry? The pothole in the street? The landlord who still hasn't fixed the heating? The boss who makes you work unpaid overtime? The local school that isn't up to the standard your children deserve? The fact that your frail father has a different care worker every week and is becoming distressed? The monopolisation of the media? The rigging of the Libor system? What's behind your anger – why do you care about these things? Where do your values come from – what are your roots? That's the beginning, that's where the drive comes from.

So I should take a moment to say what drives me and how that connects to my story. I'm a white man who went to Cambridge University. I haven't had to face the barriers in my life that many others have had to face and so my story isn't one of overcoming great personal adversity. When I first started organising I was uncomfortable with that, and tended to skip through who I was fairly quickly to talk about the issues at hand. But with time, the way that my background has shaped me and how it pushes me forward into the role that I now play has become a little clearer.

I grew up in Forest Hill, south London, in a family home that looked out over Horniman Park. My brother and I could climb over the fence and pretend that the park was our back garden. My parents, a psychologist and a psychotherapist, both worked for the National Health Service. My dad's family were working class from Shepherd's Bush – Londoners as far back as anyone can remember. My mum's family were middle class and Middle England, with roots in the north-east. They separated when I was four and divorced by the time I was seven. I was really lucky to have two amazing, caring parents and a very present dad, but my mum had to bring up two boys on her own in a single-parent household.

My brother and I went to our local state primary, Horniman's, and when it came to look for secondary schools, my mum wanted to us to be privately educated. In the early 1990s, the local state secondary school was run down and it was rough, and my mum told me later she just wasn't sure if on her own she could keep us safe and on the right track if we went there. Aged eleven, I got a scholarship to Alleyn's, a mixed private school in Dulwich. Looking back, I was so lucky to benefit from that education and that environment, but it just didn't quite fit. It's not that I felt out of place particularly, but the gap between that bubble of privilege and the reality of south London started to grate on me. As a teenager, I was mugged in my neighbourhood twice, at knifepoint; I was punched in the face several times, and I was violently carjacked. I don't want to make it sound worse than it was, but those things did happen and my brother and I were always aware in the back of our minds that kids in our area did get stabbed. But my school just seemed so pleased with itself, and it had nothing to say about any of those issues happening outside. One morning, the head actually started an assembly with: 'As I sit back in my chair and hear the crack of willow on leather [cricket], I think how wonderful it is to live in Dulwich…'

I left at sixteen and went to sixth form at a state school called Elliott. There were some really amazing teachers, but the school was coping with its share of incidents (someone being impaled on a fence during a fight and a car getting torched at lunchtime are the two that stand out); maintaining an atmosphere conducive to learning was sometimes a struggle and in some subjects, no one had got an A grade in years. My experiences in those different schools and in those different circles opened my eyes to inequality. And they haven't shut since. Some of my friends went to private school, then on to work experience with a family friend in the City – a conveyor belt to a decent university and a great career. Other friends dodged gangs in the stairwell to get home, looked after their younger sister while their mum worked nights, scratched together money for the gas meter – and then tried to do their homework. It wasn't just the unfairness that made me angry: it was the fact that as a society we say success is determined by how clever you are and how hard you work. If you fail, it's your fault. That convenient lie made me angry then and it still makes me angry now.

My roots lie in those experiences, because by then I knew what I wanted to study and knew roughly what I wanted to do. I needed to understand why young people grow up with such unequal life chances, and I wanted to do something about it. I started working on the Living Wage campaign at Citizens UK straight out of university and over the last twelve years I have been very fortunate to be building something that is making a difference. When it is tough and tiring and frustrating, I think about a few of the people I know who are now paid the Living Wage, who have dropped that extra job and can now be home to eat with their children and help with their homework. That's important to me – even more so now I have a son of my own and can see what it's like to try to balance work and children – let alone as a single parent, let alone on the minimum wage.

As you read this book, bring the things that make you angry and your own story to it. It doesn't matter if you have had to face personal hardship or not. It matters who you are, what you care about and why. These stories are what makes us human and connect us together. If we are going to build a powerful movement of people to change the world, then it's building relationships and trust around these common experiences, goals and interests that will carry us through.

The book is designed as an argument, so it needs to be read in order. Chapters 1 and 2 explore the two fundamental concepts of power and self-interest. Chapters 3 and 6 are practical chapters that contain exercises to bring the concepts and arguments to life and tools to use in your organising and campaigning. Chapters 4 and 5 are about how to develop specific goals and how to take effective action. In Chapter 7, I consider different change strategies, hear from experts in those approaches and consider how they can be combined for greater impact. Chapter 8 looks at how you can find the time to do all of this. Lastly, in Chapter 9, it's the Iron Rule of organising, and you'll have to wait and see what that is.

This, then, is a book about how to take back control. Not through a once-in-a-lifetime referendum vote or through a one-off symbolic protest, but through practical tools that can be used in your everyday life to give you more influence over decision-making and to realise your power as a citizen. These tools will help you start making the changes – big or small – you want to see. It can be done.

Chapter 1

If You Want Change, You Need Power

The Beatles said: 'All you need is love.' But they were wrong.

When you hear the word 'power', what other words come to mind? Control. Authority. Oppression. Who comes to mind? Dictators. Presidents. Media moguls.

People with strong values who believe in peace, freedom and equality are usually uncomfortable with power. They instinctively side with the less powerful in a given situation – the weak, the young, the frail, the underdog – and they dislike the powerful. They come to dislike power itself. And even if you're slightly more nuanced than that – you see that sometimes the powerful aren't that bad and that sometimes power can be used for good – would you freely admit you were hungry for power? Almost certainly not, but these strong negative associations with power actually reduce our effectiveness in putting our values into action.

Why? Because 'the standard of justice depends on the equality of power to compel'. That was true for Thucydides in the fifth century BC, and it is true now and the world over. It means that you only get the justice that you have the power to make happen, and it is the first principle of making change.

The *OED* definition of power is: 'the capacity to do something' or 'the ability to influence the course of events'. There is nothing negative about it. Nothing inherently nasty or oppressive. It is neutral. Like money. Or muscle. It can be used for good, and can be used for evil.

That issue you care about – the pothole, the social care system, the zero-hours contract – it might be the morally right thing, and it might be a good idea, but it is not going to change unless someone who has the power makes it change. It is not how right you are but how much power you have that will determine whether or not you can achieve it. Seeking power in order to make social change is not giving up on your values but being realistic about how you are going to put them into practice. Failing to seek the power you need to make those values real is just idealism. Martin Luther King Jr said: 'Power without love is reckless and abusive, and love without power is sentimental and anaemic. Power at its best is love implementing the demands of justice, and justice at its best is power correcting everything that stands against love.'

But you might still be uncomfortable. What about all those examples of people who get into power with good intentions and then lose the plot, start wars, exploit the poor and then refuse to give up their power and move on? And that famous quote: 'power tends to corrupt, and absolute power corrupts absolutely' by historian Lord Acton. But that quote is often misunderstood. He was arguing against unaccountable power, not against power itself. The context was a letter he wrote to criticise the move by the Catholic Church to enshrine papal infallibility, the idea that the pope can do no wrong, and he went on to say: 'There is no greater heresy than that the office sanctifies the holder of it.' Just as the powerful need to be accountable, those with less power need to come together to build the power needed to hold them to account.

Lord Acton is right that absolute and unaccountable power is corrupting, but so is powerlessness. It breeds fear, anger, ill health and apathy. The powerlessness of the many is just as much of a problem as the power and the corruption of the few. For both of those reasons, our democracy needs urgent invigoration. We need to hold the powerful to account and we need to build power amongst the people. The real problem about power is not that it's corrupting, but that it is so unevenly distributed. The FTSE boss and the contract cleaner. The media baron and the child refugee. The convenient myths of our current system – that democratic power is evenly distributed with one person, one vote; and that economic power is fairly and meritocratically distributed with equal opportunity to enable those with the talent and effort to succeed – mask the reality of power distribution. It's not that we are short of ideas for how to hold the very powerful to account – break up the media monopolies, close the offshore tax havens, put workers on corporate boards, and so on – it's that we are short of the power to make those ideas a reality. We get the justice we have the power to compel, and this is a book not about the big ideas for a better society, it's about how we might build power to achieve them.

The very powerful tend to have either large sums of money or positions of authority in large organisations, and often they have both. If you wish to get rich and reach a position of authority then I wish you well in that and hope you stay accountable; but those routes to power are inevitably open to a relatively small number of people. This book is about building power amongst the great majority of people in a way that is accessible to everyone and by its nature is rooted in our common concerns. It's about building power through relationships with others around common interests and shared values. It may seem weak in the face of the power of FTSE bosses, media barons and Cabinet ministers, but the power of relationships and collective action is the only defence those with less power have against the power of money and of authority. It is the victory of this people power that has brought us forward every step of the way so far in the fight for democracy and equality. So, how do we build and use this people power?

First, we must rid ourselves of the negative associations with power so that we start to want power as much as we want change. We have to spend as much time working out how we are going to be more powerful as we spend talking about what ought to be different. Second, we have to get out of the mindset and behaviours associated with the less powerful, which have been worn in through years of losing. These include:

1 Feeling completely powerless.
2 Rejecting any compromise and so choosing principled loss over pragmatic gain.
3 Stereotyping the powerful and believing your side has a monopoly on morality.

This is the mindset that we need to adopt:

1 Everyone has some power. Those with less power tend to have more than they think, or they do not use their power strategically enough. Through relationship building and the right approach you can build up your power over time.
2 Achieving social change in a non-violent way relies on politics with a small 'p'. It is the art of working with people to get the best deal you can, with the power you have or that you can realistically build. You can be clear about the lines you wouldn't cross and stick to your guns on your ultimate goals, but still make reasonable compromises to achieve some tangible progress. Compromising to achieve incremental change does not mean giving up on your ideals or sacrificing on your values. However, compromising impact for the purity of idealism means betraying those you say you're fighting for.
3 People act according to their interests and usually have a strong sense of their own morality. Relating to powerful people effectively means taking their interests seriously and respecting their values. Those who believe

they have a monopoly on morality tend to
sound shrill and are less able to move the
majority or build a powerful coalition.

So, if we accept the first principle – that we get the
justice that we have the power to compel – then it
means changing our mindset and changing our behaviour. It means spending time learning about power
– not the concept, but how it really works. Who are the
decision-makers? What would it take to move them?
It means spending time building power and patiently
and intentionally strengthening our relationships with
those who share our common interests. This involves
aligning interests with other people, joining associations and building groups and teams with those who
want the same change as you do. That's the argument.
Now let's see how it works in practice.

The first campaign I worked on at Citizens UK was
for the Living Wage. What a morally brilliant idea: a
hard day's work deserves a fair day's pay. Work should
provide a route out of poverty. And if the minimum
wage is not enough to provide a basic standard of
living, then we need a Living Wage that can.

Working with Alison, an academic at a renowned
university, we ran a research project that involved
teams of young volunteers going out to meet cleaners
in hospitals, banks and on the underground, and at
Alison's own university, asking them about their wages
and conditions of work. This produced the first list of

'targets' for the Living Wage campaign – including the university itself, which became my first organising role. Apart from Alison, I knew no one at the university and didn't have a clue how to start. The moral brilliance of the idea gets you nowhere in the face of the hard reality of trying to get things done.

The first step was to try to make contact with some university cleaners and get them to engage in the campaign. I spent a few weeks chasing cleaners – often Somali women – up and down the corridors, trying to persuade them to speak with me. I handed out flyers and I organised meetings that no one went to. I finally connected with one Nigerian cleaner called Thomas. He started to tell me what was going on. There were about 150 cleaners across the university who at £5.35 per hour were pretty much all on the minimum wage. They mostly worked the morning shift, from 5–7 a.m., with a few working through the day. Cleaners complained of being shouted at and having a tough time even getting the basic sick pay and holiday pay they were owed. The university contracted out the cleaning, so the cleaners were all employees of that cleaning company and the local manager was called Jim.

At the top of the university is the vice chancellor, running a world-class university educating thousands of young people. Down at least six layers of management, including a third-party contractor, we have Thomas and his fellow cleaners getting bad backs and living on the poverty line. Power and authority at the top and, hidden down the chain at the bottom, exploitation. The more I learned about it, the angrier I got. I wrote a long letter direct to the vice chancellor making the moral case for the Living Wage, explaining how terrible it was that cleaners were struggling on a poverty wage. But since I had no power, I received no response.

Then Thomas stopped answering my calls. I would see him across the square and he would turn the other way to avoid me. I finally bumped into him and asked why he had suddenly gone cold. He said that Jim had heard that he had spoken to me and was not only threatening him with the loss of his job but also threatening to report him to the UK Border Agency. Thomas, it turns out, did not have the right papers to be working in Britain, and in a position that vulnerable it was clear he couldn't participate in the campaign any longer. Worried about losing the only contact I had amongst the cleaners, I asked who else I should talk to – who would speak up? With the little power that Thomas had in the situation, he made a critical contribution. He recommended a Jamaican woman called Joanne, who cleaned in the humanities block.

Joanne had been working at the university for thirty years. She cleaned there when the work was contracted out for the first time and had seen five companies come and go. She knew everyone. Jim would use her to try and motivate people to work harder or to adapt to new working patterns. He might have been the boss, but in our definition, she was the leader. She didn't have the status, the salary or the position, but she had the trust of her colleagues. Jim was using her relationships – her power – for his benefit, but she was not using it for hers. Yet.

With Joanne on board, things started to move. At our first campaign meeting ten cleaners turned up. At the next, fifteen. We started collecting evidence – not only of the impact of low wages on people's lives but also information that went into our 'dirty dossier', which contained examples of underpayment, reduced numbers of workers on particular shifts and old equipment not being replaced. These sort of things were all going on below the radar; but if you looked it was there. Armed with these compelling stories we went to see various possible allies on campus and invited university academics, the president of the students' union and the trade union branch secretary to the next meeting. They heard the stories, met the cleaners and gradually came on board with the campaign.

From that point, the power started to shift: you could tell Jim was feeling it. One morning he swerved towards me in his 4x4 in a way that did not feel at all accidental. He got out the car and spoke to me for the first time. He informed me that I was barred from the campus because I'd been 'intimidating the cleaners'. Coming from the guy whose style of people management is just to shout louder – if I wasn't scared I would have laughed. I asked for it to be put in writing, but heard nothing, so on we went.

Next we compiled a video letter of talking-head interviews with the cleaners, and a whole range of allies at the university and in the wider community (including the local mosque, church and school), to send to the vice-chancellor's office. And we attached the 'dirty dossier' to really stir up a sense that this was a reputational hazard that needed to be sorted out. This time we at least got a response. The letter came back arguing that the pay and conditions of cleaners was a matter for the employer – the contract-cleaning company – and not the responsibility of the university. But we knew that as the purchasers of the contract and the beneficiaries of the service, it was the university that had the power to change the situation and the responsibility to do so.

We needed to get face to face with those at the top and turn up the heat. A march and petition was planned to coincide with the next university council meeting. For this we needed to gather together a broader coalition of allies from the campus and beyond. We mapped out the various potential networks of people and divided up the work of speaking to members of the community and inviting them along. The morning of the march we had about a hundred people and set off. At the front, leading the way, were two elderly Roman Catholic nuns. It was a slow march. Luckily we only had to walk about 200 metres to the university gates in order to deliver the petition. It worked out perfectly. The university, having got wind of the march, had overreacted and hired extra security guards with dogs. Picture the scene: two little old ladies in habits walking slowly, followed by rows of smiling students and academics, all holding mops in solidarity with the cleaners, barred from entry by a security squad with fierce-looking dogs. The local paper took the picture and ran the story with the headline: 'Nun of you can come in.'

Our campaign was given a massive boost. Within weeks we had a meeting with the vice chancellor and the university's head of finance. We found that those right at the top were horrified to find out how bad the situation had become for the contracted cleaning staff. But it required significant outside pressure to bring the issue to their attention and give the impetus for them to push through the cost and time pressures and implement changes to bring the situation back in line with the values of the university. Together, Alison, Joanna and hundreds of others on that campus and in the community had built up enough power to get into a real relationship with the decision-makers and make transformative change. The university decided to not only pay the Living Wage but also to end its contract with the cleaning firm and bring the cleaning back in-house. In one decision, 150 cleaners went from earning the minimum wage to having a Living Wage, sick pay, job security and a pension. A year later, the university won an award for social responsibility. Now there are eighty-two higher-education organisations that have followed suit, becoming accredited Living Wage Employers and benefitting thousands of people like Joanna.

There is one moment at the end of the campaign that stays with me. We were coming out of the final meeting with the university executives, at which we'd heard that the deal was better than we could have possibly hoped for. We couldn't believe that we'd finally won. I said to Joanna and Alison that it would never have happened without them, and how brave they'd been to get involved. Joanna leaned towards me and whispered in my ear: 'Thank you.'

The experience changed my life too: it made me realise that change was possible and that I had a method that could make a difference. All I needed to do was get better at using it, and start helping other people use it too. That method is what follows in this book and it all starts with the fundamental principle about the relationship between power and change – that you get the justice you have the power to compel. It is in the realisation of the central importance of power that we can shift from symbolic protest to transformative change. It's one thing to understand that you need power; it's quite another to start to build it.

Chapter 2

Appreciating Self-Interest

It's March 2015, and there are 400 people packed into Nottingham Trent University. As you look around the room, it's an unusual gathering. Yes, there are students from the university, but there are also groups of twenty to fifty people from communities across the city. Pakistani Muslims, members of the LGBTQ community, disability rights groups, the local synagogue, the Women's Centre, African-Caribbean Pentecostal Christians and so on. Up on stage, their representatives are standing together, united in a team, negotiating publicly with two politicians: the Nottinghamshire police and crime commissioner, Paddy Tipping, and Dave Liversidge, a city councillor.

The event is to launch the Hate Crime Commission report, organised by the Nottingham chapter of Citizens UK, and there are two key recommendations. First, for the city council and police to each fund a dedicated hate crime officer to take responsibility for improving responses to and the prosecution of hate crime. Second, for the Nottinghamshire Police force to recognise misogyny – the violence and harassment of women because of their gender – as a hate crime.

The evidence has been shared and proposals are being made. This team is not letting the politicians get away easily. One of the Nottingham Citizens commissioners, Sajid Mohammed, asks Councillor Liversidge: 'You've heard the evidence. Now will you fund a dedicated hate crime officer in the council who will help make sure that when people experience hate crime they actually report it and it gets responded to?'

For Sajid, it's personal. A few years earlier, his wife and child were shopping in Sainsbury's, buying ingredients to make a cake on Mother's Day, when a man shouted racist abuse at her and pushed a shopping trolley towards her and her children. More recently, Sajid has received death threats after his Muslim social justice organisation, Himmah, organised an event in central Nottingham at which they handed out roses with a message of peace.

When Councillor Liversidge responds: 'Yes we will,' the whole hall erupts in applause. The positive response is not a surprise for the Citizens team on stage. Their preparatory negotiations had been successful in persuading the council that, despite stretched budgets, this was a priority worth investing in and other councils around the country had set up similar posts, showing it could be done.

The team were less optimistic about the next recommendation. It would be a first for a police force anywhere in the country to recognise misogyny as a hate crime. Religious, racial, sectarian, homophobic, transgender, disability – these are all categories of hate crime. But not gender. And yet the local community research they had done suggested that 80 per cent of women have experienced harassment and/or violence specifically because they are female. Mel Jeffs, manager of the Nottingham Women's Centre, now asks Commissioner Tipping: 'You've heard the story, you've read our report. We are all united behind this. Will you commit to ensuring that misogyny is treated as a hate crime?'

In front of hundreds of people and the local media, it's hard to say no.

Paddy Tipping makes the commitment and agrees to work with Nottingham Citizens to become the first police force in the country to recognise misogyny as a hate crime. There is a cheer from all sides of the room. Mel and the team up on stage have smiles a mile wide.

———

That was a moment of social change. By July 2016, Nottinghamshire Police had become the first force in the country to start treating misogyny as a hate crime. By September, three more police forces were preparing to follow suit, and at the time of writing discussions are active both at the largest force in the country, the Metropolitan Police, and also in the Home Office about a national policy change. Mel, Sajid and the rest of the team have helped push us all towards a future where women and girls are safer and treated with greater respect in this country.

How did this happen? Why did that range of different individuals and organisations come together? Why did the politicians say yes?

Self-interest. It's the best way to explain how this story unfolded as it did. Self-interest is the second principle and it is the most effective way to organise people for change.

Like power, those with strong values who want to make the world a better place tend to be uncomfortable with the idea of self-interest. Surely social change is made by selfless, altruistic people who care only for others?

No.

With rare exception, people act according to what they need and what they want. And that is OK. In fact, it's more than OK: it's the only way to really engage people. So let's use self-interest to understand this story, just as self-interest was used by those who made it happen.

Sajid Mohammed came to Nottingham Citizens angry and looking for help. His wife had been abused, his children put at risk of harm, and his own life threatened. He wanted to protect himself and his family. When we unpack the concept of self-interest, we start with self-preservation: the things we need to survive – such as food, shelter and security – are the primary motivators of human action. While Sajid, like any of us, believed that all sorts of positive things *ought* to happen in Nottingham, it was the fact that he'd had a personal experience that threatened his family's safety that propelled him into action on this one. He wanted the police to do more, but he knew that to make change he needed others to help. He needed more power.

Working with the community organiser, Sajid mapped out who else would be worth speaking to, who might have an interest in a stronger response to hate crime in Nottingham. He initiated conversations. These are a few of the people he spoke to:

Stephen Legg, a geography academic at Nottingham University, who had personal experience of homophobic hate crime. Stephen had both a personal interest in a stronger police response to hate crime, so that he and other gay people he knew would be safer, and a professional interest in the idea of a community-led hate crime inquiry.

Pastor Pangani Thipa and his wife Joyce of Calvary Family Church, a community of African and Caribbean families. The couple had been victims of various types of harassment, including verbal abuse and stones being thrown; recently someone had pulled up flowers they planted outside the church and stuffed them through their letterbox. Despite reporting these incidents at various council forums, when the attacks worsened – with windows being broken and the church bus set on fire – the police could find no record of any earlier incidents.

Mel Jeffs, manager of the Women's Centre. Mel is a lifelong feminist who has personally experienced both misogynistic and homophobic hate crime. For years she wanted to find a way to get harassment and violence against women taken more seriously by the authorities.

But self-interest is not just to be found when there are fears for personal safety. People are motivated by more than basic survival needs. They can be motivated by relationships with others; by learning, enjoyment and relaxation; by a desire to live up to their own self-image and values; by seeking recognition for their identities and their efforts. As well as wanting a community in which they could be safer, Stephen Legg was interested in the way that such this community research into hate crime might connect to his academic profession; Pangani and Joyce Thipa were worried the harassment might turn people away from the church; Mel Jeffs wanted women across the country to be treated with respect because for her, being a feminist was part of her identity. These personal motivators that spur people to action are their self-interests – and we can build power with people based on these.

Out of Sajid's conversations came the idea of a hate crime commission that could bring together a wide range of different communities with shared concerns and push for a strong police and council response. The first meeting was held in a Pentecostal church, and a good number of people turned up, but the atmosphere was uneasy. The heating was broken and it was so cold that everyone sat around in their coats looking like they were about to head for the exit. And it felt like they really might leave because the Pentecostal, Muslim, disabled, women's and academic communities of Nottingham do not agree on everything and do not tend to sit round the same table. Even just being in a church was making some of the feminists and the LGBTQ activists uncomfortable. There were plenty of reasons – differences, stereotypes and fears – for it not to work and for a moment it looked like it would all unravel.

How are all these different people woven together into common action? The answer is in the community organising method at work. The first half of the meeting was one long round of introductions, based on two questions:

1 Do you have a personal story of hate crime you or someone close to you has experienced, and how did it make you feel?
2 How many people does your organisation represent in Nottingham?

The rationale behind the first question is that it draws out self-interest. People begin to share stories – of being shouted at, spat at, barged into, wolf-whistled, followed. And though the people's identities at this meeting were very different, the feelings of fear, shame, anger and powerlessness were the same. These shared human experiences cut through the stereotypes that we build up about those we don't know. People start to feel united and they start to feel angry and motivated. The question also allows people to talk about personal pain, maybe for the first time in public. And this in turn transforms someone's personal feelings into a political problem that can be tackled with others. It's been the same for the Living Wage campaign: I've heard the sense of shame in people's voices when they say they can't afford to buy their children school uniform. If you feel like it's your fault, then you keep it inside, and it eats away at you. But through organising, people connect with others and understand that their personal pain is a collective injustice, so they can stand on stage proud that they work hard to provide for their family and make a demand for change.

And the reason for the second question, about the number of people in your community? Power. Because we're only asking people to open up and share their pain because there is the potential to do something about it. If you want people to act, they need to believe that it might work. And for change you need power, so asking for numbers is a way to find out and demonstrate the potential for people power – in this case, say: 100 people connected to the Women's Centre, 500 people regularly attend the Karimia mosque, 300 members at the Calvary Church, 500 students in the university geography department … and so on. Then comes the realisation that, despite our differences, by working together maybe we can do something that none of us could achieve on our own.

That meeting in the church kicked off a community-led inquiry comprising over a thousand conversations and responses about people's experiences of hate crime. A huge amount of energy was built up through such discussions, which meant that by the time the report and recommendations were launched in front of the police and city council at Nottingham Trent University, there were already 400 people in the room who backed it.

Finding common self-interest can move people over the barriers of prejudice into coalition. Pursuing change requires us to find allies and helps us realise that our individual interests are bound up with those of other people. This is the concept Alexis de Tocqueville described in his work *Democracy in America* as 'enlightened self-interest' or 'self-interest rightly understood'. He saw it as being built up through people's experience of cooperation in local associations and as being essential for creating the feelings of broader solidarity needed for a healthy democracy. In the Nottingham example, this bond of common self-interest was developed between communities that had previously experienced conflict. As the team arrived at Nottingham Trent University to set up for the report launch, Max Biddulph, representing the Nottingham University LGBTQ network on the Hate Crime Commission, hesitated as he took out his rainbow banner. Several years earlier, he had been on the Pride march in Nottingham and was confronted by a group of about thirty angry Muslim protestors with homophobic placards. But the sustained co-operation with Muslim leaders through the hate crime campaign reassured him that their communities could stand together, and it was an emotional moment as he unfolded his LGBTQ banner and set up his stall. Several hours later, the team was celebrating a campaign success that was only made possible by connecting different communities around common interests.

However, none of them would have been celebrating if the answer from the city councillor and the police commissioner had been a 'no'. Winning is much better than losing, as any football fan will tell you. And when you're organising around people's actual problems – their real pain – then losing really hurts. If it's a symbolic protest against global inequality, where no one on the march is personally or directly affected by its negative consequences, then it's less urgent that tangible progress is made. But if you've got people talking about the time that they were scared, disrespected or assaulted, and there is one moment when a decision-maker is either going to agree to help change this situation or not, then there is a whole lot more pressure to win.

So why did they say yes? The answer, as ever, lies in power and self-interest.

There were 400 community supporters in the room; the local research had involved a thousand people; the combined membership of Nottingham Citizens is around 50,000. Covering the event at the university were the local media: the *Nottingham Post* (with a circulation of 18,000) and the BBC news show *East Midlands Today* (with viewing figures of over 300,000). Paddy Tipping and Dave Liversidge are both politicians – and politicians want votes. Turnout matters and numbers count. That's the key self-interest here.

But there's more to it than that. Politicians do care about profile and votes: they have to, as that is the requirement of getting elected, but like all of us they have stories, experiences and values that we can understand and connect to. Paddy Tipping had previous experience as an MP involved in setting up the Stephen Lawrence Inquiry into the Metropolitan Police's investigation of the black teenager's murder in south London. He was therefore already sensitised to issues around the experience of black and Asian people and the police. Also relevant to this campaign is the fact that he is the father of daughters, and we imagine he would care deeply about how women and girls feel when they are harassed because of their gender. When we organise around self-interest and look to influence people in power we have to have a realistic (not cynical) understanding of what drives them.

If appreciating self-interest can help us organise people together for justice, then why do we start off with such an aversion to the idea? Maybe when we see selfishness in the world, we automatically leap to the opposite stance and believe that selflessness is the morally superior position. We are too often taught that great people are selfless and so we should aim to be selfless too. But these days I think that selflessness is part of the problem, not the solution. I know too many people who have burnt themselves out by just giving, giving, giving – either to others or to the cause they believe in.

Appreciating self-interest is critical to successfully making change for three reasons. First, it's about appreciating our own needs and motivations. We need people who want to change the world to look after themselves so they can keep going. Second, it's about appreciating the self-interest of others. People who just go round trying to sell their pet issue and bang on the same old drum are not going to bring large numbers of people together. We need to be genuinely interested in other people, find out what drives them and how we can find common interests and common ground. Third, it's about recognising that people are motivated to get involved by the things they care deeply about

– such as their families, jobs and neighbourhoods. It is a mistake to expect other people to commit to a cause above the things that are most important to them – family, work, rest and so on. We need to turn that thinking on its head. It's not despite people's interests that they're going to get involved – it's because of them. Social change needs to be something the majority of people can participate in, rather than being the preserve of saints or superhumans. It takes time and energy to fit meetings and events into our already busy lives. So if people are going to get involved and stay involved, it needs to be about something that really matters to them.

One of the clearest signs that you've totally failed to connect with people's self-interest is when you hold a meeting and no one turns up. I thought that I had learnt this lesson as a rookie organiser, but I got a cold, hard refresher just a couple of years ago in Sheffield. I walked into the Circle – a nice venue I had booked for a meeting on the upcoming general election – and spoke to the guy on reception.

'Oh, Citizens UK, yes, we have your booking for 7 p.m. Great to meet you, we've heard of your work. Have you come up from London today? Yours is Room 3 and we've laid out thirty chairs with tea and coffee.'

By 7.10 p.m., it was still just me sitting on my own in Room 3.

The nice guy from reception comes along.

'Hi there, just checking if you're OK, maybe people are a bit late ... don't worry.' He was being nice, which made it worse.

When I walked out of the place at 7.30, with not a single person having turned up, he looked at me pitifully, but tried to add brightly: 'Never mind – it does happen. Back to London this evening?'

A low point. With ten years of organising experience behind me, how did I get myself into that embarrassing position?

Because I had been taking too many shortcuts. In the previous months there had been a decent listening campaign and engagement process with Citizens UK member communities in the cities and towns where we had a real presence. Together we had created a manifesto for the upcoming general election. In those areas we were holding events for between 100 and 2,000 people because people had been involved in the process. Then we took that manifesto out to marginal constituencies around the country, where we didn't really have an existing network, and tried to round up a local team of people to meet with the parliamentary candidates. Sheffield was one such marginal, and my responsibility. I had sent maybe twenty emails to different people telling them about the Citizens UK manifesto, telling them how important these issues were. Social care, asylum seekers' rights: surely they care about those things? People said they might come. I didn't speak to anyone face-to-face, and I didn't try to find out what they really cared about.

It should have come as no surprise, therefore, when no one turned up. It just wasn't in their self-interest to do so. They had no ownership of the issues or the strategy on offer and they had no relationship with me. I don't want to be in that situation again – and I wouldn't want you to be either. So that means taking seriously other people's self-interest.

To bring it back to the core argument: if you want change, you need power. You build power through relationships with other people and those relationships are built around mutual self-interest and common goals. Now, power and self-interest might sound uncomfortable, but it's through this lens that we can best understand how politics works and the levers that can be used to make changes happen. At a deeper level, the practice of building power with people who are different from us breaks down prejudices and creates trust. As we start to interact effectively with the decision-makers and those in positions of power, we realise that they also act on a combination of narrower and broader self-interests, and that they can be trusted as much as anyone.

Rather than cast blame on out-of-touch elites, the onus is on us to work out what we want, to get organised and to build the power in order to get it.

Chapter 3

Practical Tools to Build Power

This is not a book about how the world could be. It's not about abstract political theory or how the parliamentary system operates. It's about how you can make a difference to the things you care about. So, as well as the argument and the concepts, there are tools and tips for what you can actually do.

These are the three tools to put the concepts of power and self-interest into practice:

1 The stick person
2 The one-to-one conversation
3 Power analysis

They might seem a little unusual at first, but you'll probably find you're already doing this kind of thing intuitively in the way you live and work. These tools are just a more elaborate and explicit version of people's day-to-day political instincts and activities. You will already be thinking about what people care about and tuning your interactions with them accordingly; you'll be having conversations with people to connect with them and work out how to cooperate together; and you'll be analysing where power lies and how to get things done. These tools will help you hone these political instincts and increase the chance of you making a difference.

THE STICK PERSON

The stick person is a tool towards a greater appreciation of self-interest – your own and other peoples' – and it can be used to help build relationships around common interest. In my introduction I asked a simple question: What makes you angry? The question is a quick way to find out what people might be motivated to take action on, and in community organising we ask it a lot. Did you have an immediate answer? Maybe you had loads. Maybe you weren't sure. The stick person is a way to develop a richer understanding of self-interest than any one question can reach. If you weren't sure of an answer to what made you angry, or struggled to choose between several, then the stick-person technique will map out your different interests and something will emerge. If you already know what you want to change then the stick person exercise will help you connect it to the place it comes from and where it fits in your priorities and your story. Sustained motivation comes from a deep sense of who you are and why you care about things. It will take 30–45 minutes and it's best to do it in a quiet place on your own.

Draw a stick person (that's you in this first instance) and start to list around it the things that are important to you, using these prompts:

(a) Who are the people most important to you?
(b) What are the institutions and places most important to you?
(c) What are the moments and stories that make you who you are?
(d) What are your core values?
(e) What are your central concerns?
(f) How do you spend: (i) your time (ii) your energy (iii) your money?
(g) What are the things you wish you could change if you had the power?

Don't just rush through. Take some time to think.

Now you've got it down on paper, what was surprising to you about the process? What did you learn about yourself? Do you think that your priorities have changed since you last really thought about these things? In fact, when did you last think about these things – maybe you never have? Do you take your own interests seriously enough to really think them through? Are you spending your time, energy and money around the things you really care about?

Working through these kinds of questions on your own, in silence, can be a profound experience. When we run this session on our residential training courses we have had people totally reassess their priorities, quit jobs, call up loved ones to apologise, and decide to dedicate themselves to making a difference.

But the stick person is not just a tool to reflect on your own interests. It's a tool to help make an impact on social change. It challenges you to really get to know what drives the people you want to work with so you can build a relationship based on common interest. How detailed a stick person could you create for the people you work closely with? Could you do one about your boss? Or your MP even? Do you know their roots, their key ambitions? Try and make their stick person and see how well you do know them. In a campaign, we could and should spend time researching about the issue, the costs and benefits, but always remembering that decisions are taken by people who have a whole range of personal and organisational interests. This tool helps to map that out.

THE ONE-TO-ONE CONVERSATION

It starts with what you care about, the thing that will drive you into action. But it can't end there. Building power with people means connecting your interests to their interests. If you want to really understand another person, what they care about and why, that can't be done through an online survey or by gut instinct. Building the kind of relationship that will stand the tests of working together for change can't be done by emails. So what's the answer?

Face-to-face conversations. This is the most important tool in community organising, and I'm afraid there are no shortcuts. It means taking time with people – making people and relationships the priority – even when it feels there's no time and you just need to rush on. There are also fewer barriers. This method is available to most people. It doesn't require money or a special qualification or technical expertise. Most of us can have conversations with people and build up their power this way. What I mean is a specific type of conversation, and there is a real art to doing this well. You can get better and better at it with practice and with coaching. To distinguish it from other conversations, we'll call it 'the one-to-one'.

It's good for:

- Building strong public relationships that will endure.
- Understanding what really drives people and what they care about.
- Sharing what's important to you, finding areas of common interest and planning collective action.
- Identifying talent, leadership and useful networks.
- Agitating people to act around the things they care about, and challenging yourself.

Dos	Don'ts
Go into it intentionally – because you think there's some common interest, talent, knowledge, or network of value	Pick random people and chat aimlessly
Ask the person what they care about, their story, values, interests, aims	Sell your issue
Share what's important to you – your story, values, interests, aims	Interview the other person
Push the person to take a risk and take action around what they care about	Annoy people by telling them what they ought to take action on, if they don't care about it

Dos	Don'ts
Have a 50:50 balance in who is speaking and who is listening	Dominate the conversation
Aim for collective public action rather than sympathy and support	Have a therapy session
See it as a way to find and connect with the right people and to creating ongoing productive relationships	See it as a one-off and then return back to the emails and the same old task-oriented meetings

Just a side note about the lingo and setting up these meetings.

Here it goes:

Ring ring. Ring ring.

'Hello?'

'Hi, my name's Matthew – Annie recommended I get in touch with you about this social change project she said you were interested in.'

'Oh yes, I know Annie. How can I help?'

'Well I want to book a one-to-one with you so we can build a *relationship*.'

It sounds dodgy. In fact, it sounds a bit like you're asking them for a date. (We have had at least one marriage – congratulations Gunther and Julie – that came from the one-to-one conversation, but that was a happy side effect.) This tool is about public relationships for collective action, so it's generally best to avoid saying 'one-to-one' or the word 'relationship' and sounding like you're on the pull.

Instead, 'Could we book a coffee so I can find out more about what you're interested in and share what I'm doing?' will do nicely.

The one-to-one conversation is a tool to purposefully build up strong relationships. It's a route to power that is available to practically everyone; power with others for change.

POWER ANALYSIS

'But I don't have the time to go and have conversations like that with everyone.'

No, you don't. So you have to be strategic about who you're going to build relationships with and how you're going to build up your power. Be intentional about what kind of change it's worth your while putting your time into: what's achievable, and how you could influence those decisions. The tool to help with these sorts of questions is the 'power analysis'.

Everyone has an instinctive power analysis in a given context. We can name who we think is the most powerful person:

'The prime minister makes the big decisions on
     UK energy policy'
'At work, my boss is the one with the power'
'What grandma says about Christmas, goes…'

And we can mostly say whether we currently have the power to make something happen or not:

'I can choose to move to a renewable energy
supplier. But I can't get the UK government
to double investment in wind power'

'I can take a day's holiday pretty much whenever
I want. But if I want to book two weeks, I
need to convince my boss that my work will
be covered'

'I haven't got a hope in hell of persuading
grandma not to boil the sprouts until they're
falling apart…'

Developing a more sophisticated power analysis has
three advantages:

1 It challenges any mistaken assumptions in
   our initial understanding. The official organisational chart – the organogram – doesn't
   contain the real detail on when and how
   decisions are made. But who sets the agenda,
   where are the real deals done that get rubber-
   stamped at the official meeting? Who are the
   players who might not have formal positions
   but have influence?

2 It helps us analyse the dynamics around any
   key decision-maker. They may be the most
   powerful person, but they are also likely
   to be extremely busy and to rely on other
   people around them. They are accountable to certain rules and institutions, and
   they are themselves working to maintain
   their power amidst changes in the power
   dynamics.

3 It opens up the horizon of the change you think is possible. Just because you don't have the power to do something right now – 'it's out of my hands' – a more sophisticated power analysis enables you to develop a plan for how to build up allies, change the power analysis and win.

Most importantly, the power analysis offers a way to map out your existing relationships and be clever about how to build up your power and make the change you want.

So start with a power analysis of the most important and relevant organisation or network you are part of. This might be your workplace, union or industry association, a neighbourhood association, a school, faith group or residents' association, a national charity or campaign organisation. Pick one that feels worthwhile, that you want more influence in; that could help you make an impact on what you care about. First start to map out where power lies:

(a) Who are the five most powerful people?
(b) Who controls the money?
(c) Who are the leaders with the strongest relationships?
(d) Which important sub-groups are there and who leads them?
(e) How do decisions get made? How do they really get made?
(f) Who are the most senior people accountable to?

Then consider your own power in it:

(a) Do you have formal decision-making power?

(b) Do you know the people you listed above? What influence do you have with them?

(c) How many people do you know? How strong are your relationships?

(d) If you wanted to change something small or big, could you do so? Who would you need on board?

Now comes the key question: how can you gradually build up your influence in that setting? Who do you need to build relationships with in order to gain power? These are the people to have one-to-one conversations with and to connect around the interests that are mapped out on the stick person.

These three tools work together to help people build people power and get you ready to make change. But there's one more critical step before we get to action.

Chapter 4

Turning Problems into Issues

Turning problems into issues is perhaps the clearest piece that is missing from the symbolic protests – and it is a critical step in turning people power into change. The big cause needs to be broken down into specific issues, giving a greater chance of success and a platform on which to build more power and tackle bigger issues.

Thinking about the problems of the world can be depressing and disempowering: poverty, climate change, education inequality, racism. I can worry about them. I can talk to my friends in the pub, and I can post my opinions on social media. But I can't do anything about them until I break them down into issues. Climate change is a big problem. But if my aim is to get five friends to use a renewable energy provider, this becomes a solvable issue. Five people using green energy will not save the planet on its own, but neither will another discussion with the same environmentalists about why people should just all suddenly see how important the problem is.

It's not about losing sight of the big problem – it's because we care about climate change that we are compelled to break it down into something we can tangibly affect. And it's not about just taking the easy route. If we've got the power to achieve big change, then let's aim big. But there is no point in pretending we have the power to solve the problem in one go, only to make no difference at all. When breaking the big problem down into an issue, we are aiming to choose something that is significant and ambitious enough to be meaningful and, based on a power analysis, has a decent chance of being winnable.

Achieving the specific issue makes a difference, albeit a partial one, and in this example five people have chosen to use renewable energy. But, just as importantly, with each small success comes a sense of accomplishment and motivation. Maybe the next step could be that each of the five people encourage five others, and then together you could all persuade your local MP to back an upcoming bill in Parliament to invest in renewable energy. It's a strategy of incremental change where the aim is to move from smaller to more significant victories, and to get more effective and build relationships as we go.

The Living Wage provides another example. The stories and experiences that gave rise to the campaign in east London in 2001 were those of parents not having time to spend with their children because they were forced to take on two, sometimes three, jobs because rates of pay were so low. Here 'working poverty' was the big problem. But what could parents and communities do about working poverty itself? They could moan about it, raise awareness about it, pray about it. But they couldn't tackle it until they turned it into an issue. The Living Wage is a number (then £5.80 per hour) and any given employer either pays it or they don't. It's not just about having a specific aim, it also requires focus on a particular decision-maker at a specific place and level. Our campaign didn't start off, as is so often the case, thinking that the government needed to step in and legislate. It was about that group of people with their concerns, persuading local employers to pay a decent wage. It was tangible and winnable, but not easy. It took two years to persuade the first hospital and three years to persuade the first bank. However, with each victory the power of the campaign and the pressure on others to follow suit increases.

It sounds straightforward, but the problem is that many people who want to make a difference are idealistic: they want to move from where we are now to where we ought to be in one go. They've spent years dreaming of a better world and a small incremental step in that direction feels such a long way off. That's how I felt coming out of university. I still felt the injustice of the wildly different lives experienced by children in south London, plus I was equipped with all the radical theories from a social science degree about how things should be.

The reality of making change hit home for me when I attended my first London Citizens action. I showed up bang on time at the meeting point, St Matthew's church in Brixton, one Wednesday afternoon in 2003. What was it going to be about, I wondered – racial injustice, or inequality maybe? I was excited to be part of something radical, so it was a bit of a downer when I realised the aim of our action that day was to get Lambeth Council to agree to a review of public toilet provision in central Brixton. I sat there hearing the stories. Without any public toilets in the area, people would come out of the nightclubs in the early hours at weekends and relieve themselves anywhere – on church steps, in shop doorways. The next morning people would turn up for church or go to the shops and have to wade through urine. I felt doubly uncomfortable. First, because I thought I was signing up to change the world and here we were talking about public loos. And second, because just the previous weekend I was at one of those nightclubs (the one actually in the old church called Mass, which ran drum and bass nights) and I wondered if I had been one of the culprits.

As we walked down towards the council offices, I dutifully took my turn carrying the porcelain toilet that we were using as a none-too-subtle prop for the action. It was even heavier than you might think, but by the time we reached the council building I was more concerned that my mates would see me standing by a toilet bowl on a street corner, holding a placard calling for 'More Loos'. Very soon another demonstration appeared, also choosing Lambeth town hall as their location; three people each carrying a placard with the more inspirational slogans of: 'Peace', 'Equality', 'Justice'. It crossed my mind that I might be better off with them, but before I could think more about switching allegiances, the relevant Cabinet member came onto the council steps and there and then agreed to the 'loo review' and to a meeting within the next two months to discuss the situation in detail.

As a result of the action, a pilot scheme was introduced and temporary toilets installed to monitor the amount of urine 'delivered' per day. A full community scheme was announced (the research reinforced the community's experience that there was indeed a lot of wee), with twenty-five participating businesses opening up their toilet facilities for the public to use. The council made a further commitment to ensure that you are never more than 500 metres from a public toilet in a town centre in the borough of Lambeth.

You might think toilets aren't important – but for people who are older or have illnesses or disabilities, access to toilets can be a major barrier to venturing out. Plus, let's be honest, when you're desperate to go, finding a toilet is the most important thing in the world. Either way, the success of the toilet campaign helped people build their power and their confidence to be more ambitious. Lambeth Citizens went on to win campaigns for the Living Wage, to control payday lenders, to welcome refugees, and much more. There may be a seductive appeal in one great moment that changes the whole world, but in my experience it is incremental steps that edge us closer to the world as it should be.

———————

The image of the three-person demonstration on Brixton Hill, with its noble aims of 'Peace, Justice, Equality', came back to me several years later when I saw the nine-point statement made by Occupy London in response to the banking crash and subsequent 'age of austerity'. These are three of the points:

1   We demand an end to global tax injustice and our democracy representing corporations instead of the people.
2   We want structural change towards authentic global equality.
3   We call for a positive, sustainable economic system that benefits present and future generations.

When you first look at these, they seem inspirational and radical. But then you think about them again, and who would disagree? They are so broad and so vague that I bet you would have more than half the FTSE 100 chief executives and nearly all the MPs in the Commons agreeing to them. They are not focused enough to land responsibility at anyone's door and not specific enough to really know whether we are making progress. As has been mentioned, despite huge media attention, there was no discernible impact from the Occupy London protests on tax, equality or sustainability and the failure to turn problems into issues was one of the reasons why.

Contrast this with the agenda that London Citizens launched at the Barbican in 2009, at their 'Citizens' Response to the Financial Crash' assembly:

1   Employers to pay the Living Wage of [then] £7.60 per hour to all employees, including

      those working for on-site subcontractors,
      starting with the Corporation of London.

2 The government to introduce a 20 per cent
    APR cap on personal loans to control exploit-
    ative payday lenders.

3 The government to introduce a series of
    regional endowments to fund community and
    small business development, capitalised by 1
    per cent of the funding reclaimed from the
    bail-out (approximately £10 billion).

So, what impact is made possible by focusing on specific issues? On the first point about the Living Wage, Mark Boleat, then deputy chair of the Policy and Resources Committee of the Corporation of London, was present at the assembly and had to make a public response. There's no vague statement of principle that can avoid the clarity of what a properly defined issue requires – which is a yes or a no. And in the case of Mark Boleat on that day, he gave a positive commitment and agreed to work together. The Corporation of London is now an accredited Living Wage Employer, benefiting hundreds of low-paid workers and showing an example to the many big businesses located in the City.

On the second point, it took a lot more campaigning by Citizens UK and other partners to persuade the government to control exploitative payday lenders with an interest-rate cap, but it did happen. In the end the Financial Conduct Authority decided on a cap not of 20 per cent APR, but of 100 per cent TCC (total cost of credit). Though this wasn't exactly what we were after, it has had a hugely positive impact, outlawing a huge swathe of exploitative lending offers and benefiting hundreds of thousands of people.

On the third point, we weren't successful at all. It was specific enough to count as 'an issue' in this definition, but it was too ambitious a proposal and was an overestimate of the power of Citizens UK that we might be able to persuade the government to commit such a massive amount of investment into regional endowments.

So, turning a problem into an issue is no guarantee of success by any means. But failing to turn problems into issues greatly reduces the likelihood of any tangible impact. When I see events designed to raise awareness, or big marches with broad vision statements, I just wish there were some specific issues in there too so that the pressure could be felt and some change made to happen. So if it's so important, and may seem obvious even, then why does it not always happen? What are the barriers and how do we overcome them?

Problems lead to conferences and issues lead to action. Throughout school and college we are taught to be 'students': to analyse and to argue, to make the case for and against. We are not taught to be 'citizens': to practise the art of politics, the tussle of making change and the reality of making compromise. We have spent years in institutions where analysis and conferences are the criteria of success.

Problems lead to conferences and issues lead to action. The great advantage about sticking with problems rather than cutting into issues is that you can talk about problems all day. Poverty is a problem. It's so complex and multifaceted that it requires a lot of analysis. More discussion and more research. Let's hold a conference. Everyone can come and agree that poverty is a big and complex problem that requires … further thought.

I was almost put off the idea of democratic action altogether by student politics. One meeting was about global trade injustice. Someone had suggested that we persuade our university to adopt Fair Trade. We spent the first hour debating whether the word 'trade' was already sacrificing our principles because it was all about monetary value rather than people's intrinsic value. Then we spent the second hour arguing whether the Fairtrade mark was strong enough: shouldn't we be making our own mark? Then we spent the last hour, as people wandered off, arguing about whether the coffee growers in Columbia were actually being held back more by a corrupt government and should we campaign for that instead. Too many meetings wasting all that time and energy discussing and amending motions about issues that they will have zero influence on. No one cares if you are for or against if you don't have a plan to take action and make a difference. We were mimicking the rules of the game from academia – where it's good if the outcome is more discussion and more analysis but no action.

Now there is social media to reinforce the tendency to analyse and argue: it has set up a whole lifelong world of opportunity for being opinionated about the problems without ever taking action on the issues. Whether we are in an echo chamber agreeing with each other, or getting into pointless arguments with people we will never meet, it doesn't make any actual difference to decision-making and outcomes. It merely gives the appearance of political engagement while reinforcing divisions but without compelling people through the tussle and compromise of political action.

The second reason people tend to steer away from turning problems into issues is that they feel uncomfortable with the real-life tension and confrontation that comes with the specificity of 'an issue'. No one (and everyone) is responsible for the inequality that results from the global capitalist system, whereas trying to get the Living Wage for the hundred or so men and women who clean up when the conference is over is an issue. The principal of the university will either pay it or they won't. It's an issue that there's going to be some conflict about, because it's real and tangible. The aversion to conflict is as true for individuals as it is for certain organisations. For example, if an organisation is funded by the government, it's easier to organise conferences and discussions about the problem rather than break it down into issues where government ministers might suddenly be held to account.

Finally, some people seem to have found a strange solace in losing. It's usually born out of idealism combined with powerlessness, where people come to enjoy the moral high ground of losing. It goes something along the lines of: 'I have such high principles and the world is so corrupt that losing just proves how right I am and how wrong other people are.'

One way to overcome such barriers is to start with the tangible and visceral substance of self-interest. Start with what is really happening to people who are present, rather than with a discussion about theories, principles or issues people have read about in the news. For Rosa Parks, for Abdul Durrant, for Sajid Mohammed, and for the people that know or knew them, it isn't about some vague sense of how the world ought to be; it's personal. The physical presence of someone who stands to lose or gain serves as a strong driver to push a situation from talk into action. Any campaign that doesn't have people who personally, depending on the outcome, stand to benefit or suffer can get lost in the angst and worry of problems, rather than the clarity of issues. It's also a very good idea to get people in the campaign on the same page about the approach, recognising the principle that we only get the justice that we have the power to make happen. Then the need to pick a winnable issue will be clearer, and the discussion can be about strategy, rather than an abstract debate. This of course applies at the level of any campaign team and at the wider scale of our democracy, where we need a society-wide effort to educate people as citizens in the practice of politics, rather than just the study of it.

Lastly, it's important to say that even if everyone's on board with the need to turn a problem into an issue, there's a real art in doing it in the right way and at the right time. Large numbers of people are more likely to gather around a compelling problem or vision rather than a smaller, specific issue. So one way is to keep the overall 'brand' big and broad, and then focus on some specific proposals within it. Make Poverty History is a good example. The brand and vision was wide-ranging and compelling enough to recruit hundreds of local organisations into a coalition and over 200,000 people into action at the G8 Summit of 2005. But there was – absolutely – a specific issue at the negotiating table: the 0.7 per cent target for government spending on international aid (which the 2017 Conservative government has just recommitted to). Applying this to a local campaign, it is usually best to start off with a series of conversations and events about the bigger problem and engage people that way, building up power and recruiting people to the group or cause. By doing this you can invest time into building relationships and trust between people so that when you start cutting the problem down into winnable parts, and prioritising some areas over others, you can survive the tension and tough decision-making that goes on in trying to choose the right issue.

Of all the experiences I have had of trying to turn a problem into an issue, the most painful and profound was the Citizens UK Strangers into Citizens campaign. The campaign sought a one-off regularisation for some of the 1 million or so undocumented people living in the UK. Just getting the campaign supported inside the Citizens UK membership was a real struggle in itself. Many people started off with the strong feeling that illegal immigrants were not deserving of citizenship and that to campaign for them to have a chance for permanent residency would reward illegality and put additional stress on scarce resources.

The turning point in getting agreement for the campaign internally came not through a policy discussion of the economic or security benefits of regularisation, though of course we made those points in the campaign. It came when we created a space where people within the member communities could speak out and explain: 'It's me and my family we are talking about. You have seen us, you know us, but we are living in fear every day.' People heard the stories of parents who had been living and working in the UK for years, with children in school, worried every day that their families would be uprooted and their children's futures thrown into turmoil. People who had fled war and poverty in their countries to seek refuge in Britain, who were stuck for years in the limbo of the asylum system, without the right to work. And others who were being exploited financially and sexually by employers and landlords, but who couldn't then go to the police.

Individuals such as these took huge personal risks by participating at the heart of the Strangers into Citizens campaign. It was their stories that built consent and created the energy for action, and they were involved in the problem-to-issue process. We knew that to stand a chance of being successful we couldn't campaign for every undocumented person to have permanent status in the UK, as we knew how difficult it would be to persuade the government to act at all. So we had to cut the issue down to what we thought might be achievable and that meant including certain groups and not including others. Being involved in those discussions for the people who had irregular status that meant the difference between a chance of safety and a hopeful future and no chance at all.

In the end, through many difficult days of discussion, we opted to focus on those people who had been in the UK for a minimum of seven years, even though this excluded thousands of people, some of whom were right at the heart of the campaign. Two things stick in my mind. One is the dignity with which those people who stood to lose out accepted the political necessity of cutting the issue down. The other is the moment when one Zimbabwean failed asylum seeker called Anthony, who is disabled through polio, made a compelling argument that we should include a condition that undocumented migrants gaining regularised status would not be able to claim benefits for a qualifying period of two years, as he thought it would make the issue more winnable. Generally, I found it was people who had 'irregular' status themselves who were the most prepared to compromise access to any state support because they were so angry at being portrayed as scroungers and so desperate to come out of the shadows. But in the end it was largely the voices of people who were not in the situation themselves but for whom this idea of temporarily limiting benefits went against their principles that won out, and Anthony's suggestion was not included in our final campaign proposals.

The time spent building up internal support and listening to each other's stories meant that the campaign coalition stuck together through this difficult process of deciding the issue. Amidst a series of campaign events and tactics, we held a mass rally of 20,000 people in

Trafalgar Square and managed to secure support for 'regularisation' from the *Guardian*, *Independent*, *Economist* and *Daily Telegraph*. In terms of impact, the campaign did help push the government towards fast-tracking the asylum 'legacy cases' – those that had been stuck in the Home Office system for many years – towards rapid and almost entirely positive decisions for an estimated 160,000 people. However, we didn't win the larger campaign on irregular migrants. Hundreds of thousands of irregular migrants are still living in fear and at risk of exploitation.

Did we cut it right? Should we have included Anthony's uncomfortable but pragmatic suggestion? Did we underestimate the forces up against us? I've spent some time soul-searching, but the point is, it's better to try; you celebrate the successes where you get them, and you don't give up. We are now back tackling the problem with a more specific issue, looking at increasing the number of children without status gaining permanent residency, and working on the issue with the Mayor of London, Sadiq Khan.

So, turning problems into issues is a crucial step in any successful campaign. If the problem is not broken down, it is intangible, overwhelming and too big to solve. Winnable issue by winnable issue we can build up power. It's not always easy, but the process of discussion and deliberation, of working out what power we have, what compromises we would be prepared to accept, is an important democratic practice. It requires trust and relationships of the sort that are just not possible in the one-off symbolic protests that rely on rapid mass mobilisation and a loose coalition.

Building power through relationships and turning problems into issues together helps people develop political skills and gets us ready for effective action.

Chapter 5

The Action is in the Reaction

Let's recap the argument. Start with what makes you angry. If you want change, you need power. You build up power through relationships with other people based on common self-interests. You break the big problems you share down into specific issues – and then you're ready for action. Action is what turns people power into change.

People often hear 'action' and they think 'protest'. But protest sounds like you're reacting to someone else's agenda – they have the power, they are calling the shots, and the people scramble together a protest. Like resistance, it sounds reactive. Action is different. Action means the people have a plan. They are initiating the change and someone else is going to have to react. Action doesn't have to be a standard form of protest, like a demonstration or a march. Action can be very different: tea parties, carol concerts, report launches, flash mobs, public assemblies, collective clean-ups – the list is never-ending. It is not about the form the action takes or necessarily the size (though numbers are important); it is about what it achieves, about what reactions it provokes.

For all the million different actions and different factors that make an action work or not, the best place to start is with Saul Alinsky's simple maxim: 'The action is in the reaction.' There are two meanings to be drawn from it:

1 Action should be planned and then judged on the basis of achieving certain reactions.
2 The less powerful side can influence the more powerful by taking an action that prompts an overreaction.

The first point forces us away from symbolic protest: just making a statement about what we believe in because it's the right thing to do. That's not an action planned to achieve a specific impact. If we consider, for example, the Occupy London movement of 2011–12: for all its laudable aims, we are forced to assess it on tangible results. These were not a reduction in global inequality, but the resignation of St Paul's Cathedral clergy. Regardless of the intended focus, it was actually amongst the cathedral staff that the greatest tension was felt, as they struggled to find a balance between supporting a well-meaning protest and getting the camp out of the way to allow access to the cathedral. Using 'the action is in the reaction' assessment, we must judge the campaign harshly.

The second point is a more sophisticated take on the tactics of effective resistance. When people with less power are up against serious institutional or financial power, 'the action is in the reaction' encourages the weaker side to provoke some kind of overreaction that can be used to strengthen their campaign or undermine the authority. An illustration of this would be the Living Wage action, where the university responded to a slow march led by nuns by sending in extra security guards with dogs. It was this overreaction that made the university look a little ridiculous and more swiftly led to negotiations that achieved a victory for the cleaners. Between these two examples, the fundamental lesson is in turning symbolic protest into action for power and change.

To draw out some principles of effective action, let's go back to the moment when Abdul Durrant stood up in the HSBC AGM and said directly to Sir John Bond: 'We work in the same office but we live in different worlds…' Why does that story stand out? You can imagine what it's like on a normal day in the two wildly different lives. Abdul travels to work by bus because he can't afford the tube, wearing the uniform of the contract-cleaning company, and arrives at 11 p.m. to clean through the night. After eight hours of wiping desks and mopping floors, he leaves at 7 a.m. to make his way home and try to sleep, with all the worries that come with attempting to provide for a family on just £5 per hour. And just as he is leaving, Sir John Bond arrives for an early-morning meeting in a chauffeur-driven car, sitting comfortably with a £2 million per year pay package, plus use of a private jet, private dental treatment and the rest. They pass in the corridor with a polite nod. The gulf in power could not be wider. But in the AGM, the power dynamics are turned upside down. Abdul is a shareholder, with the formal right to hold the CEO to account. He is dressed smartly and sits there with his team. He stands up and tells his story, and his simple truth cuts straight through twenty layers of hierarchy. He explains what he wants and, while the cameras click furiously, he asks for a meeting, which he gets, and creates a connection with the person with the power to make the change happen.

What can we learn from this? First, it shows that breaking the problem into issues and doing a power analysis are both essential preparation. The action wasn't about a general problem of inequality or working poverty in London; it was about a specific pay rise for a particular group of people, and the decision to focus on the banks meant that it was deemed winnable – they could hardly say it was unaffordable. The power analysis showed that, although the employer was a contract-cleaning company, the power lay with the client bank: HSBC set the procurement policy and tender, which the contractors then competed with each other to win, usually by keeping costs and cleaner pay as low as possible. The target for the action was therefore the chairman of the bank rather than the cleaning company itself.

From what took place at the AGM, we can draw out four components for effective external action:

1 There is confrontation. The action creates a
   moment where the decision-maker is forced
   to confront the issue and, if possible, the
   person experiencing that issue. Creating a

confrontation is not about aggression. It is about creating a civil moment when conflicting interests are made public in a way that subverts the normal power dynamics. In this instance, Abdul was both a cleaner – lowest in the hierarchy – and a shareholder at the AGM. The chairman – highest on the hierarchy – is accountable to the shareholders.

2 There is recognition. The campaign gets noticed. More than that, the decision-maker is compelled to recognise the person. The HSBC action captures the deeper meaning of the word 'recognition' (from the Latin 'to know again') perfectly. Sir John Bond knew Abdul before as a face, as a cleaner, but through the action Bond had to 'know Abdul again' for who he was: a father with a name, a citizen with some power, and a shareholder.

3 There is tension. Change requires tension. It's worth noting the reason for the AGM action was that HSBC had refused to meet to discuss the Living Wage. At various stages during the two years it took to persuade HSBC to change their policy, they said that the Living Wage was illegal and unaffordable. The kind of tension I'm talking about is definitely non-violent and, in my experience, it's better to be overly polite in a way that contrasts with the injustice being exposed. Just for Abdul to be there, to contrast his life with Sir John Bond's, was enough to introduce huge tension and move the campaign forward.

4 There is a relationship. Just as relationships between people are what build up people power, we are also aiming for relationships with the decision-makers. Protests that just take place outside of the decision-making can have an influence, but if we are interested in making some specific tangible change, it's best to get in there and negotiate for it. In this instance, the AGM action was enough to get a meeting. But it took multiple meetings with HSBC staff, and several further actions, to keep the tension up, to get a victory. And sometimes the relationship might develop in ways you wouldn't expect. When Sir John Bond came to a Citizens UK assembly a few years later, he said that his meeting with Abdul was one of the most important moments in his time at HSBC – and when Abdul applied for a job as a trade-union organiser, it was none other than Sir John Bond who wrote him a reference.

The action creates a moment for a new sort of relationship to be struck, and when it's the less powerful side trying to influence and hold accountable the more powerful side, picking the right time for the action is key. For publicly listed companies the AGM is a good time, when the board and executives are physically present and to be held to public account by shareholders. For politicians, the weeks before elections are the time when they are most actively looking for votes and keen to make public appearances. This creates a great opportunity for action and influence, but it's one that is often missed, not because people do nothing, but because in what people do, there isn't the strategy required. Take the traditional hustings occurring in nearly every constituency up and down the country. What tends to happen? People trickle into the church hall – thirty on a bad day and perhaps a hundred on a good day. The vicar welcomes people in and says how important democracy is and thanks the politicians for coming. Each politician gets five minutes to make a stump speech with some combination of policy and criticism of the others, and then there are questions from the floor. Fine. It's not the politicians I'm frustrated with. It's the people. They are disorganised. It's mostly just individuals asking their own personal questions. Each question is as important as the next and as soon as it's asked, it's gone. Don't get me wrong, a hustings is better than nothing, but there has to be a more powerful role for the people than just that.

What if instead of showing up just to hear what the politicians have to say, you organise a delegation of, say, twenty people to go to the hustings who all stand up together to politely but purposefully ask a specific policy question and include a request to meet the politician afterwards to discuss it further? Or what about if the team organising the hustings itself decides that it isn't a chance for politicians to tell people about their manifestos, but the other way round? What about if it is the people setting the policy and asking the politicians to adopt it?

Well, that's the thinking that goes into a Citizens UK accountability assembly. It's often mistaken for a hustings, but it's trying to create a different relationship between politicians and people. The big difference is that the people have organised in advance and worked out what the collective agenda is. The event is then planned so that the questions being asked are policy proposals on this specific agenda, not random questions from the floor. The politicians are invited to give public responses – including a clear 'yes' or 'no' to whether, if elected, they would support the proposals – and the people will do whatever they can to hold the politician to these commitments. It's strictly non-partisan and the aim is to get the candidates to support the policies of the people, regardless of their party. Numbers do matter in an assembly such as this, because politicians and their teams are constantly making calculations about votes. Elections can be won or lost on a few hundred votes, so even if it's only a hundred people at the event, taking this sort of action instead of attending a traditional hustings can make a big impact.

The largest assembly we've pulled off was for the 2016 London mayoral elections. Over 6,000 people from London Citizens gathered in the Copper Box arena of the Olympic Park – young and old, different faiths, ethnicities and backgrounds, all united behind a common policy agenda that had been developed over the previous year. In the Citizens manifesto were seven specific proposals around affordable housing, youth employment, wages and integration. The policies were brought to life by testimonies given by people who had helped shape the proposals. One was a sixteen-year-old from Abbey Wood, southeast London, called Dylan.

He described how rising housing costs had forced him and his family to move five times since he was eight years old. That's why we were asking for a Good Development Standard that would ensure 50 per cent affordable housing in new developments, or that planning permission would require a tough public scrutiny of the developer's plans to show why this was not possible. The biggest round of applause was for 21-year-old Ijeoma, who had been living in London since she was two years old, only to realise, when she hit eighteen, that she did not have citizenship, which put her whole life in limbo. That's why we were asking for the creation of a deputy mayor for citizenship and integration, to promote citizenship registration for young Londoners. Before looking at the impacts of the action, it's worth examining how this kind of assembly tried to create a different kind of democracy.

The two leading candidates, Sadiq Khan and Zac Goldsmith, both attended and respected the process of the assembly and each other. This was in stark contrast to aspects of Zac Goldsmith's media-oriented election campaign, which included making spurious and divisive insinuations about Khan's supposed links to extremism. The 6,000 Citizens were respectful too, cheering when candidates made positive statements about policies, with no booing or jeering at any point. People were angry about the housing crisis but they were dignified and purposeful in trying to do something about it.

The BBC was present, filming all night, but on the evening news just three seconds of footage of the Assembly was used, as the backdrop to another story altogether. Former mayor Ken Livingstone had made allegedly anti-Semitic comments and had been suspended from the Labour Party. The choice of top story was disappointing to those involved, but wasn't a surprise. The media representation of our political culture tends to feature personality over policy, and conflict over constructive engagement. No matter that Ken Livingstone had not held office for eight years, or that six thousand Londoners had gathered in the biggest event of the election – it is politicians and celebrities who are portrayed as the significant political actors. Ordinary people tend to be left to the role of spectators – maybe tweeting a view or featuring in a five-second vox pop, but mainly just faces in a crowd.

On a more positive note, at the end of the assembly we made a commitment to be at London's City Hall and to bring breakfast to the mayor and his staff on his first day in office, to congratulate whoever was elected, and show that we meant to continue a working relationship that would see the policies delivered. When newly elected Sadiq Khan met us that Monday morning and took a croissant he said: 'You've kept your promise to me to bring breakfast, and I will keep my promises to you.' For someone who had just been put in charge of a multibillion-pound budget, with all the responsibility and pressures involved, that phrase captured very well the kind of democratic culture we were aiming for: organised citizens working with accountable politicians. A year later, there is now a deputy mayor for social integration, social mobility and community engagement, promoting citizenship registration for people like Ijeoma as one of their top priorities. There is a new housing policy aimed at ensuring a minimum of 35 per cent affordable housing in new developments, with public funding aiming to raise it up to 50 per cent. Such policies will help people like Dylan and his family find genuinely affordable homes to call their own.

At the time of writing, we have just had a general election and, while another vote may come a lot sooner than the five years of a fixed term, the political reality now is a hung parliament with a Conservative minority government. This means that just a handful of MPs voting one way or the other could make all the difference, and individual MPs' ability to make amendments and do deals on local issues is increased as government aims to secure support and pass legislation. With the prospect of an election looming, MPs will want to strengthen their reputation and increase support among their constituents now more than ever – so this is a great moment for action and influence by the people. Whether your aims are national or local, you can get organised and lobby your MP to support you. The whole method outlined in this book applies, as in any campaign, but here are five specific tips for having effective influence on your MP:

1 Build a team or join an existing organisation to find allies and build your local power. MPs care about verified local voters so it does matter that your team and your allies are from the constituency.
2 Find a good source of information about when critical votes will be taking place in the

Commons so you can time your interactions and requests. Research the interests and the voting patterns of your MP to understand more about what's possible and how to make the case.

3 Always ask for something specific, for example: voting one way or another, making or supporting an amendment or convening a meeting of local decision-makers.

4 Your MP's office will read and usually respond to communication, so a series of letters or phone calls will show them that people care about the issue. The more personal the communication the better: make it clear that it's from a constituent, with a specific proposal, and always request a response. If they don't respond then ask again, make a complaint public on their social media, and if that still doesn't deliver then plan action to increase the tension.

5 MPs regularly attend local events that provide opportunities for action and a face-to-face encounter. If you are using the opportunity of an event on a different topic, then do be respectful and creative about the way you turn the focus to your issue, because you ultimately want to meet with your MP and get them on board.

6 MPs care a lot about local press coverage, so with some public action and a good local angle it should be easy enough to get your issue into the newspaper.

Keeping on the theme of taking action to influence politicians, the campaign to push the Living Wage right into the heart of Westminster – and so begin its rollout across the rest of the country – provides an example of risk, failure, perseverance and impact. From the outset the same 'David and Goliath' potential was there, as it had been with Abdul and Sir John Bond, because the prime minister and all the secretaries of state have people who clean their offices: the country's most powerful politicians in close proximity to the minimum-wage workers who clean the loos. We put time into meeting with Whitehall cleaners, hanging around outside service entrances and jumping on the bus with them as they went to their next job, just to catch ten minutes with them. We had to raise hopes enough that they would come to our meetings, sign letters, speak to the press and ultimately put their jobs on the line for change.

We started back in 2008 with a march around Whitehall, delivering petitions to government ministers signed by cleaners and Citizens UK members. There was one significant success that got the whole thing rolling. In response to an impending article in the *Guardian*, a Department of Education press officer made a statement that the Living Wage would cause inflation and put people out of work. It was a mistake on their part but a great opportunity for our campaign. For a start, the department had actually signed the Child Poverty Pledge, which recommended paying the Living Wage – so it was hypocritical. Second, all we were asking for was for a few cleaners in the Whitehall department office to be paid £1.50 per hour more, so the idea of inflationary pressure was totally overblown and appeared ridiculous. In the *Guardian* article covering the action and reaction, Ed Balls, then secretary of state for children, schools and families, was attacked by unions on the left and by Conservatives on the right. It made him look foolish and he promptly moved around fifty department cleaners onto the Living Wage.

It was our first Whitehall victory. Encouraged by it, we carried on. We spoke to more cleaners and organised more marches and petitions. The government changed in 2010 to the Coalition, and after David Cameron called the Living Wage 'an idea whose time has come' at a Citizens UK assembly before the election, we began some detailed conversations with Treasury special advisers. We quickly realised, however, that we were getting nowhere and needed more outside pressure. So in the summer of 2011, we organised another march around Whitehall: but again no reaction. This time we marched with mops and buckets, but these started to feel like cheap gimmicks rather than clever props. It's not fun when you're not winning.

Worse, we heard that managers were hassling staff they'd identified as being involved in the action, and cleaners were losing patience. Katy Rojas comes to mind, an Ecuadorian woman working as a cleaner at the Foreign Office. She had been fighting for the Living Wage for several years, speaking at events and persuading her colleagues to sign letters. 'But how can you expect me to persuade them to sign another letter when nothing happened from the last one? I am in debt myself, it's not getting any better,' she said. I started to feel like a fraud. We had to do something different.

We wanted to try and create the Abdul Durrant–Sir John Bond moment, the confrontation that gets into the papers and cuts into the public consciousness. But there were no AGM-type events and it was almost impossible to get the schedule of any given secretary of state long enough in advance to organise for a cleaner to be there, let alone ask a question. But the cleaners did work in the same offices and pass the same politicians every day. They literally worked on the same desks.

The idea finally came in a meeting with the cleaners and a journalist. They could leave a letter directly on the desk, from the cleaner to the secretary of state, asking for a meeting. In its politeness and simplicity, it turns the massive power imbalance on its head. The huge hierarchy between them vanishes in the simple civilised request for a meeting from someone you pass every day but never speak to. And what decent person could turn that down?

I remember sitting in a café on Caxton Street in May 2012 with 'Marissa', a cleaner who worked in the Department for Work and Pensions. We were both scared. She had the letter in her hand and we were discussing how she should deliver it without getting caught. Marissa had two daughters, she was already struggling to make ends meet, and she knew as well as I did that this could put her job in jeopardy. She was telling me why she was doing it: for herself, for her colleagues, and for her daughters to know that she was a fighter. We hugged as she left the café. It was a long wait.

When she returned, the words came out in a rush I could barely understand. She did not have the pass to access the Secretary of State for Work and Pensions,

Iain Duncan Smith's, office. So she'd waited to one side until someone came out of the room, darted across and slipped inside to leave the letter there. The daring but simple act was reported in *The Times* and within a couple of weeks we had a date for the cleaners to meet with the secretary of state.

Why was Iain Duncan Smith such a good route in? Self-interest.

First of all, he had a strong policy interest in the Living Wage. The Department of Work and Pensions was at that stage under huge pressure to reduce spending, putting at risk Iain Duncan Smith's flagship Universal Credit programme. Every person who got paid the Living Wage would save the DWP money in tax credits; so it was in the secretary of state's interest for it to spread and become government policy. Second, we judged that the Living Wage would resonate with his personal story and values. Iain Duncan Smith was committed to 'making work pay' through a combination of his values as a Catholic and a transformative experience he had had visiting a deprived part of Glasgow, where he met people on benefits who felt that moving into work would make them worse off. However, even with those self-interests present, it still took the action – the letter-drop and *The Times* newspaper report – to actually get the meeting with Iain Duncan Smith. I remember the email that finally clinched the meeting: '*The Times* journalist wants to know if the secretary of state is refusing to meet his cleaner.'

Change requires tension. It's so difficult just to get noticed and to get your issue anywhere near the top of the pile when powerful people are facing so many competing pressures for their time. We had to make it urgent, and we had to make it relevant. In the meeting that followed, I remember, one cleaner called John told Iain Duncan Smith: 'My back is getting very painful from the work. My wife tells me I'm stupid, that I should quit and go on benefits because we wouldn't be any worse off. But I don't want my sons to ever say that their dad didn't work.' Following that meeting, Iain Duncan Smith, to his credit, broke ranks amongst his Whitehall colleagues and began implementing the Living Wage across the DWP, bringing Marissa and hundreds of her colleagues a 25 per cent pay rise. He also crucially began pushing it strongly at Number 10.

Six weeks later we worked with Whitehall cleaners on a simultaneous letter-drop on the desks of ministers in eight other government departments. We had coverage in the *Evening Standard* and on *Newsnight* and we started to get replies from ministers and permanent secretaries, with some departments starting to move to the Living Wage. With the DWP and other departments breaking from the pack and moving to the Living Wage, it enabled us to start to set up and publicise over the next couple of years the Whitehall Living Wage League Table, ranking secretaries of state against each other in terms of treatment of their lowest-paid staff. In July 2015, the government announced the 'National Living Wage', which, although less than the real Living Wage, has brought significant pay rises to over 2 million people, including nearly 700,000 care workers, with some who were stuck on the minimum wage getting a 10 per cent increase.

There were many factors at play, but the actions of Marissa and others – the very brave and simple acts of leaving letters on desks – played a significant part in making this happen. I'm glad I have had a chance to tell their part of the story. Change doesn't happen in one moment. It's about how we build from one small meeting to the next and how we find new ways to put pressure on those who can make the change we need. It's about planning a strategy several steps ahead, where an action is designed to elicit a reaction, or an overreaction, that helps strengthen our hand and provide the context for a bigger action. This did happen in the story of the Whitehall cleaners, but we weren't ready to fully grasp the opportunity. One unintended reaction of the second round of letter-drops was that a cleaner, Valdemar, who had dropped the letter on the minister's desk in the Cabinet Office, was subsequently moved to another site by the cleaning company and lost a considerable amount of pay. It was a foreseeable reaction and I kick myself still for being unprepared to respond swiftly. In the end we managed to organise pressure to help Valdemar end up with a positive outcome, but we lost the campaign opportunity to respond immediately and publicly to the cleaning company's overreaction.

The example from history of 'the action is in the provocation of an overreaction' that has inspired me the most took place in Selma in 1964–65. The account that follows is a simplified version of a more complex reality.

Despite the 1964 Civil Rights Act, which in theory ended discrimination on the basis of race and would enable African Americans to vote, in many areas this had made little difference to actual voting numbers due to various bureaucratic barriers, plus outright intimidation. Martin Luther King Jr and key leaders from the Southern Christian Leadership Conference and the Student Nonviolent Coordinating Committee were working on a strategy to win a much stronger Act and were looking for a place to make the focal point of the campaign. They selected Selma in Dallas County, where only 300 out of a possible 15,000 African Americans had managed to register to vote. The Governor of Alabama, George C. Wallace, was steadfastly pro-segregation and the local Dallas County sheriff, Jim Clark, had a reputation for violent conduct towards African Americans. It wasn't the fact that Selma was a place where the problem was at its worst that made the civil rights campaigners pick it. It was the fact that Selma was a place where they thought they could prompt an overreaction from the authorities and enable an escalation of the campaign that might create the energy and urgency to move the president, Lyndon B. Johnson.

Through January and February 1965, there were small protests and marches. On 26 February an Alabama state trooper shot and killed a young African-American demonstrator, Jimmie Lee Jackson – the first, tragic overreaction from the local police. A march from Selma to the state capital of Montgomery took place in response to this killing on 7 March. Under the policing of Sheriff Clark and Governor Wallace, a peaceful march of 600 men, women and children became violent, as protestors were brutally attacked by troopers wielding whips and nightsticks and firing tear gas. The scenes were broadcast on television and this grotesque overreaction by the authorities brought in further activists, civil rights leaders and religious leaders of all faiths in their thousands to Selma. A further protest planned for 9 March was halted early by Martin Luther King Jr and other leaders in the face of another likely brutal response by the police. Civil rights leaders and supporters called for federal action on protection for the Selma marchers and also for a new Act to guarantee voting rights. As tension rose, there was another killing by segregationists – this time the victim was a young white minister, James Reeb.

The local struggle became national news and impossible to ignore. President Johnson intervened to guarantee the safety of those marching and on 21 March, 25,000 people, under the protection of 1,900 National Guard, marched from Selma to Montgomery. Public opinion had been changed and by August 1965 the new Voting Rights Act was passed, prohibiting racial discrimination and lifting many of the barriers that prevented equal access to the vote. It was a strategy. The less powerful side planned ahead, working out how their initial action would provoke an overreaction that would make the opposition look terrible and galvanise their own supporters, building up their power and enabling them to take a larger action and ultimately to win.

There is a radical history of people power, action and change in every region and through every decade, once we open up our eyes and take an interest. My favourite park, Queen Victoria Park in Bow, sounds by the name like it was the result of a generous royal bequest. In fact, it is the result of people power and action in what was an impoverished part of the capital. In response to the smog and ill health of nineteenth-century industrial London, and the fact that there were plenty of royal parks in west London and none in the east, a petition of 30,000 signatures was collected and local residents marched directly to Buckingham Palace to demand a park for east London. The campaign was successful and just seven years after Queen Victoria Park was finished, the Chartists started using it for mass political meetings.

Stories such as these can be an inspiration and an example as we plan our own actions, build our own campaigns and start writing our own chapters in history.

Chapter 6

Practical Tools to Build a Campaign

The point of this book is that you can make change happen. It might start small; you may not be playing the lead role, but that's exactly what is needed. More people doing a bit more. That's how the big changes happen – through lots of little changes. So the last thing I want is for you to get to the end of the book and think: 'That all sounds interesting enough but it doesn't help me on the thing that I want to change.'

This is the second practical section and it gives a summary of the key steps in the development of a community organising campaign, along with some tricks of the trade. Don't get put off if some of them don't seem to fit your situation, and if you already have an ongoing campaign with a different approach, then use the bits that do apply and don't worry about those that don't. If it's not clear how to move from one stage to the next, then go back to the last practical section. The fundamental tools at work all the way through this are the stick person, the one-to-one conversation and the power analysis.

Community organising moves through a cycle of research to action to evaluation. It's never neat and there is no single path to follow. It's a craft, and most of the time you don't know whether it's going to work. But you keep going. And that's exactly how all the great stories of social change have begun. There are three things to consider about the overall mindset:

1　The method is there as a basis for experimentation.
2　Prioritise relationships and keep learning together as you go.
3　Have a laugh as you do it, particularly when it gets tough.

I'll lay out the steps and then run through each piece in brief. There are three sections with a few steps in each:

Research

1　Build or join a team
2　Run a listening campaign
3　Arrange a collective decision-making event

Action

1　Internal action
2　External action
3　Turnout

Evaluation

1　Learning
2　Celebration

To help illustrate the techniques, I'm going to describe a real campaign story alongside the method. The story is of a young man called Ismael Musoke who was born in this country, but went back to live in Uganda for most of his childhood. When he returned to the UK aged seventeen, he knew no one; he was shy and quiet, and struggled to feel at home even though it was his home.

The story starts with Ismael in Coulsdon College, Croydon, and a chance meeting with a Citizens UK community organiser, who asked him what he was worried about and what he wanted to achieve. Ismael said he was worried about finding a job and that he was angry about his experiences of discrimination. He said he wanted to feel like he belonged, and he wanted to make a difference. The organiser suggested he come to the introduction training happening the next day in the college.

RESEARCH

Build or join a team

'Never doubt that a small group of thoughtful, committed citizens can change the world. Indeed, it is the only thing that ever has.'[TM*]

MARGARET MEAD

*Used under licence from the Mead Trust

The starting point is always to get a team together. At the beginning it might be small, just a few people, but that's a start. The team gives more skills, more time, more knowledge and more networks. Also, you're probably doing this in your spare time, so life's bound to get in the way at an important moment, and you'll need cover.

Here are some basics of a good team:

1 Around eight to fifteen people, to allow for a third not to be able to make any particular meeting.
2 A range of skills and access to different networks.
3 A clear allocation of roles.
4 A culture of action and accountability.

The one thing I would emphasise most is to nurture the relationships and nourish the motivation. The relationships are what holds the team together and motivation is what drives it forward. There are two simple ways you can do this:

1 Start meetings with rounds of introductions, where people share something personal and relevant about the issue at hand, and asking: 'Why is this issue important to you?' This constantly reinforces the motivation and opens up personal information for people to develop relationships around.
2 Eat together, have fun together and encourage people to meet for one-to-one conversations.

So, back to the story. Ismael attends the community organising training and gets hooked. At that stage he has no position, no status and very little power. But the method offers him a practical way that he can build up his networks and his influence, develop his skills and maybe tackle the things he cares about. He does a power analysis and realises that one way he can increase his power is by running for president of the students' union in the upcoming college elections. He has one-to-one conversations with some of his friends and classmates to build a team: in building this small team – about five students – he's really connecting into their interests in developing employability skills and experience for their personal statements, rather than anything grander, at this stage at least. They agree to help him with the election.

Run a listening campaign

When you first hear of a 'listening campaign', you'll understandably think of something that sounds similar, like market research, a survey, or a needs assessment. The crucial difference in a listening campaign is that we are doing two things together:

1. We are finding out what people care about – their self-interests.
2. We are building the power of people to make change.

Which means that at the end of the listening campaign you have:

1. An issue (or set of issues/manifesto/priorities) that has come from people, or common self-interest.

2 A body of people who have the ownership and the power to drive forward the project and campaign to make it happen.

The difference cannot be overstated. If you just conduct a survey, then there's no more capacity to tackle those issues than there was at the beginning. Although people have been consulted on what they think, they're not the ones with the ownership, responsibility and capacity to do something about it. On the other hand, the listening campaign aims specifically at building the power of people to uncover and tackle the issues they are facing.

The listening campaign is about enabling people to voice what they care about and engage them in making the change happen.

1 With the team, map out the neighbourhood or the community that you're going to be listening in. If possible, weave the listening campaign into activities that are already happening, in order to reach more people and save effort.
2 Use a power analysis to work out any particular leaders or networks that need to be included.
3 Practise your story about why you're doing this – why the listening is taking place, what the parameters are – so that it becomes clear, but also motivates and inspires others to get involved.
4 Your team is developing their leadership through these conversations and is also

looking for leaders. If people stand out
because it seems as though they care and
they're connected, then challenge them to
become involved and to bring others.
5 You're also looking for emotive stories.
When it comes to the internal decision-making actions or the external making-change
actions, these stories will motivate people.

The team needs to plan the listening campaign together.
Also, try to keep at least one step ahead of the process
so you know where the listening is heading and so you
can invite people to the next action.

For Ismael and his team, the listening campaign is
the only hope of success. He is up against a much more
popular student. The usual students' union approach of
putting up posters and speaking at one or two hustings
is not going to work for him. No one knows his name;
he needs another way. He puts his recent training into
practice and maps out the student body, including the
leaders and influencers in each class. He and his small
team run a listening campaign of face-to-face conversations – five to twenty minutes each –with over 300
students in a four-week timeframe. Through these
conversations the team expands from five to fifteen
students: people who care about the issues (crime,
employment, public transport) but who are not being
engaged in the normal run of the election process.
Usually, it's just a bit of a popularity contest and then
not much happens as a result. This way, when students
voice their problems, they are challenged to be part of
the solution.

Arrange a collective decision-making event

The most important thing you're doing through the listening campaign is building power and energy. So it's important not to lose it. The listening campaign culminates in a collective decision-making event where all the people doing the listening, and many of the people being listened to, come together. This could have the feel of a conference or a community festival, depending on your context (but, generally speaking, give me the community festival any day).

Collective decision-making creates ownership around the priorities and the upcoming action. We want to move directly from the listening to the collective decision-making and into action without losing energy. It's an art to get it right in each context, but we can generally think about a two-stage process. The first one involves people feeding back the issues and concerns they heard in the listening campaign and agreeing on some top priorities. Then some more research is needed to turn those problems into issues and prepare a strategy, including the public action.

For Ismael, there are two significant decision-making events. One is in his college and involves about thirty students bringing together the results of the listening campaign in order to decide the manifesto he will run on. 'Youth employment/work placements' heads the results and by the final week of campaigning, Ismael is running on a top issue that he knows is deeply felt. Plus, when it comes to the events and hustings, he has real and compelling student-based examples to offer. The network created through the listening campaign helps Ismael's team turn out the vote. He wins the election by a small but significant margin and becomes president of the student union. Ismael has accomplished part of what he set out to achieve: he's known around the college and he's more confident; but he also actually wants to make a difference. He has raised the hopes of his fellow students that something's actually going to get better in terms of youth employment and work placements. The problem is that the post of student president – with a tiny budget and some access to the college hierarchy – is not going to deliver the changes he seeks. He needs more power and he needs allies.

The second decision-making event is a Croydon Citizens assembly, where groups of people from local schools and churches come together to decide on their common priorities to put to the politicians in advance of the upcoming local election. Ismael brings twenty-five students from Coulsdon College to the assembly and together they present a proposal for a project called First Step Croydon, which will deliver a hundred new student work placements. The proposal is voted onto the top four issues going to the politicians. As Ismael and his team celebrate, they make a pledge that around fifty students will attend the next big Citizens assembly, where hopefully the politicians will agree to support the First Step project.

ACTION

This section is about the strategy of action. It's more of a mindset and a habit than a particular type of event. How do we use action to build power and to make tangible change for the things we care about? What are the reactions we are looking for and how do we craft the action accordingly?

Internal action

Particularly at the beginning of the campaign, internal actions are good to build capacity. The listening campaign and decision-making events are internal actions, and then further internal actions help keep the energy up through the campaign and reach new people. For example:

- Organising community-based activities that are fun and accessible and engage people who might not get involved straight away in the campaign as such.
- Weaving the campaign into existing events and connecting the issue to existing priorities and traditions.
- Sharing emotive stories about the problem you're tackling in order to get people interested. Listening to people about their concerns.
- Having a series of possible actions that people can take, starting small and building up.

External action

External action is when the power you've built up in your campaign is used to influence decision-makers in other organisations to deliver the change you're seeking. Usually, the action is about getting a more powerful person to recognise you and your issue, and establishing

a relationship where negotiation can take place, leading
to a deal. Unless it's something they're already on board
with, it's going to require respectful confrontation and
constructive tension, which is always a careful balance
to strike. Across a wide range of possible situations,
here are some tricks of the trade:

1 Being close counts. If they won't come to
   your event then you need to go to them, to
   their HQ or to a high-profile event.
2 If you can't act directly on them, act on their
   revenue streams or who they're accountable to
   – investors, advertisers, target voters, govern-
   ing bodies, regulators, media, etc.
3 Pick a time when the target is most able to be
   influenced, for instance when they need the
   support of the people, just before elections,
   at AGMs, or when they are launching new
   initiatives or big events.
4 Personalise and polarise. You can't take an
   action on a system where everyone and no
   one is responsible. You have to focus on a
   named person who can make the decision,
   and in that moment, on the specific issue;
   it's right or wrong, not a grey area. In that
   moment, they have to choose.

Overall, any one action is part of a strategy of building power and making incremental change. Action
causes reaction to lead to your next action, so it's about
planning ahead and being ready as a team to learn and
adapt.

Turnout

There's one component of an action that's important enough to deserve its own section. If it's people power that we're using to make change, then numbers are important. I don't mean a one-off mass mobilisation of 50,000 people because of a social media thread. I mean the ability to regularly turn out something between 30 and 300 organised people who are all in agreement about what's trying to be achieved. If the room is virtually empty then all the reactions, internal and external, will be negative. Really simple stuff, but it's important:

- Make sure people come because someone they know has invited them with a decent reason for why they need to be there.
- Focus on the leaders who can bring their followers.
- Build up towards bigger events with smaller ones, where people make a public pledge to attend the next one.
- Be realistic about event venues and numbers: better to have a room for 50 with 60 people in it than a room for 150 with 70 people.
- Make events enjoyable and meaningful and always make sure they end on time, otherwise people might not return.

Ismael and his team did bring nearly fifty students to the Croydon Citizens Assembly, and with close to 250 people in a hall in Coulsdon College, with only a couple of weeks to go before the election, the politicians turned up and gave mostly positive pledges to the team's proposals. The councillor leading the Labour group, Tony Newman, said yes to the proposal for First Step Croydon, and so when he became leader of the council, Ismael and his team already had a partner in the local authority. The team asked the council to use their networks and influence to engage businesses in the work-placement scheme, and to give some of their staffing resource to making First Step work.

On a Thursday afternoon in July, Ismael and his team worked with the council to bring twenty Croydon employers together with forty young people to launch First Step. After lots of young people had talked about their motivations, their skills, their hunger to learn, and the council had talked about how it would lead by example and offer placements, each employer had to pledge the number of work-experience placements they would offer. It was going fairly well – pledges of 2, 5, 3 placements – and they were building up towards the magic target of one hundred. But then, speaking last, the CEO of the large insurance firm Allianz Global Assistance, Serge Corel, stood up. He looked Ismael in the eye and said: 'This is not how it works in business; if I give work experience placements, I give them to the children of my friends. I'm afraid I can't pledge anything.'

No one expected that and no one quite knew how to react. The event carried on, but all of the positive energy had disappeared and it ended on a low note. Ismael and the team thanked the businesses that had come, cleared up the hall and gathered together for the evaluation. Ismael felt he had one chance to make sure the disrespect that the team was feeling didn't descend into despondency or rage, but could be channelled into something positive … and he did.

EVALUATION

Evaluation is about creating a campaign for change that learns as it goes along and about creating a group of people who grow in their understanding about what works and what doesn't.

Learning

At the end of every action, from the big events to the small meetings, there's an opportunity for learning. We do it orally and in the moment, because the aim is to get an immediate sense of the reactions we've drawn out, what's working and what we need to do differently. Here are some common evaluation questions:

- Q. How do people feel? – When the change is driven by people power, feelings matter. We are constantly mindful of the levels of energy and hope, because that's what fuels people and brings people back.
- Q. What reactions were we after and did we achieve them? If not, why not?
- Q. What did we learn?
- Q. Who did well? Who didn't do as well as they hoped? – This is about a culture of recognising people's efforts and being accountable to each other on the roles people played and whether

we brought the number of people we said we would.

Q. What are our next steps? Given the reactions we caused, where are the opportunities for action?

And so, what happened in the evaluation at the end of this story of Ismael? The feelings were understandably very negative: 'angry', 'deflated', 'humiliated'. The outright refusal by Mr Corel had upset the team. They saw that kind of nepotism as exactly what was preventing them and their friends from getting decent jobs. With the energy of the campaign, and the trust of his team at stake, Ismael spoke up and said: 'We'll show him what young people in Croydon can do.'

The following Monday, the team had organised forty-five people, dressed in smart business clothes and holding their CVs, to queue up outside the Allianz HQ near East Croydon station. As the students handed in their CVs to the reception desk, they said: 'I just wanted Mr Corel to know that young people in Croydon have got talent and we are ready to work.' The action was covered in the *Croydon Advertiser* that day and within two hours Allianz got in touch with the offer of a meeting with Mr Corel. Ismael and the team negotiated for Allianz to offer work-experience placements and for the students to be paid the London Living Wage.

Celebration
Celebration is a step that's all too often missed because we're often focused on the issue and maybe feel like

we're swimming upstream. But that's all the more reason to celebrate the small successes and celebrate each other. It's the relationships and motivations that carry us through and that need nourishing.

Cue celebrations with pizza for Ismael and his friends. First Step Croydon continues to grow and offer young people in Croydon their first quality work placement. Ismael Musoke went on to lead a Young Citizens assembly in advance of the 2015 general election, and Allianz Global Assistance is now an enthusiastic partner in the employment scheme.

Chapter 7

Unusual Allies and Creative Tactics

What do you do if you follow those campaign steps and you still can't win? This chapter is about going beyond the usual suspects to find unexpected allies, and combining creative tactics to get the impact you're after.

Every time you get on a bus you are experiencing the results that come from the power of unusual allies. The disabled people's movement in the UK had campaigned for fifteen years to persuade the government to introduce the Disability Discrimination Act of 1995. But they were sorely disappointed with one significant omission: transport provision. The bus companies had lobbied hard to exempt themselves, saying that to widen entrances and make other adjustments for wheelchair users would be too costly. Rather than give up, disability campaigners teamed up with women's organisations who had a common interest in accessibility – getting their pushchairs on. This alliance created the extra power to push government to overrule the bus companies and now we have buses that are accessible to wheelchair users and to parents with prams.

Moving beyond the usual suspects is also at the heart of the Living Wage story. One key driver of success has been the alliance of the moral force of faith and the economic credibility of business. 'Bishops and business' was Stephen O'Brien's (former Citizens UK trustee and founder of Business in the Community) catchy phrase. The faith leader says: 'This is about doing the right thing, it's about dignity. There are parents in our communities who are working two jobs because the pay is so low, and they are unable to look after their children.' The business leader says: 'This is about responsible business, it's our company values. By paying a Living Wage we improve our retention, productivity and reputation.' By keeping these two voices front and centre of the campaign, through events and communications, we have made the Living Wage impossible to ignore and difficult to dismiss. Contrast this with the Living Wage movement in the US, which has ended up, almost without exception, as a pitched battle between, on the one side, trade unions and community organisations, and on the other, employers and business lobbies. This means that it tends to follow politically partisan lines, with Democrat politicians supporting the Living Wage and Republican politicians against – who can much more easily say: 'It sounds like a nice idea but I'm on the side of business and the Living Wage will kill jobs.'

A turning point for the campaign in the UK came when Boris Johnson was seeking election as the Conservative candidate for Mayor of London in 2008. Gaining the support of the previous mayor, Ken Livingstone, had been a major step forward for the Living Wage campaign, and if we lost that mayoral support then the whole thing could have been derailed. Boris Johnson, standing for a party that in 1997 had battled against the introduction of the National Minimum Wage, was faced with a choice. A choice he would have to make publicly in front of 2,000 people, plus BBC London and the *Evening Standard*, at the London Citizens Mayoral Assembly, just one week before the vote. Would he say yes or no to supporting the Living Wage? To say no, he would need to make the case that it would be bad for business, but he was up on stage with five big-name employers proudly making the case that the Living Wage was a fantastic thing and had all sorts of business benefits. And so it was a resounding 'yes' that evening from Boris Johnson to the Living Wage, and once elected he did follow through with that commitment, paying it to thousands of staff across the Greater London Authority and banging the drum successfully for the Living Wage at events and in newspaper articles. In that moment, the UK Living Wage movement added a third B to its unusual alliance: 'Bishops, business' and 'Boris.' The combination of faith, FTSE companies and a prominent Conservative politician meant that the Living Wage could not be dismissed merely as a preoccupation of those who might be deemed the usual suspects – anti-poverty charities, left-wing politicians or trade unions.

By 2014, this had become an unusual alliance that Prime Minister David Cameron was finding it hard to ignore. The Leader of the Opposition, Ed Miliband, had made the Living Wage his flagship policy; the Living Wage Foundation, set up by Citizens UK with the support of Mike Kelly at KPMG, had now accredited its thousandth Living Wage Employer, including a quarter of the FTSE 100; and Boris Johnson was in the press every week as a Conservative leadership candidate as well as a Living Wage champion. It had become impossible to justify opposition to the Living Wage, and by organising the Whitehall cleaners to drop letters on ministers' desks we were creating moments when the issue was pushed into the media spotlight and the government was forced to respond. I don't know the exact combination of reasons that led David Cameron and Chancellor of the Exchequer George Osborne to introduce the National Living Wage in 2015, and we only got a phone call from Osborne's office twenty minutes after the announcement, but it was in response to this pressure that our campaign for a Living Wage moved a Conservative government to make the biggest increase to the legal minimum wage since it was introduced in 1997. Depending on your background and tastes (and your stereotypes) you might find either bishops, business or Boris a little unpalatable – or maybe all three. But in April 2017, this unusual alliance had enabled several million people to get a pay rise. So, being strategic and pragmatic, who would be the unexpected allies in your cause?

Again, this is about more than just campaign strategy. If governance is about warring political parties scoring points off each other in the media, while we boo and cheer, then it does not build collaboration and trust between people. But if politics becomes a pursuit of the people, then the practical demands of seeking change are to put away some of those prejudices we all have, and to find common interests with others, including those we disagree with and those in positions of power. That's why populism by the people can be the antidote to division and distrust rather than its cause.

As well as unusual alliances, we need to use creative tactics. You've heard of a 'sit-in', where some campaign group makes their physical presence felt by temporarily occupying a meeting or building. Well, Saul Alinsky famously planned the first ever 'shit-in', where busloads of campaigners would take over all the toilets in Chicago's O'Hare Airport for a day and bring the whole place to a standstill because none of the thousands of passengers had anywhere to relieve themselves. The action was nothing to do with the airport itself: it was an outlandish attempt to bring a resistant Mayor Daley back to the negotiating table on issues affecting poor neighbourhoods in the city. The airport was the Mayor's pride and joy, and Alinsky reasoned correctly that such absurd scenes of disruption, with all the press coverage and ridicule they would generate, would be too much for Daley to bear. Fortunately for the airport passengers, the protest was never actually carried out because the threat of it alone was enough to get the Mayor back on side.

There are plenty of examples of audacious and radical tactics here in the UK that were carried out and did make an impact. The founders of the Salvation Army were husband and wife William and Catherine Booth and one of the social injustices that angered them was the sexual exploitation of children, which was rife in the East End of London, where they were based. The practice was partly enabled by the fact that the legal age of female sexual consent was then thirteen years old and in 1884, despite efforts to have it raised to sixteen, it appeared that the relevant amendment would not be passed by Parliament. Catherine Booth and the Salvation Army decided to act. Within just a few weeks they had – incredibly, in the days before online petitions and emails – raised a 250,000-strong petition. However, they knew that more sensational action was needed. In partnership with the *Pall Mall Gazette*, Catherine enlisted the help of a reformed prostitute to procure a girl of thirteen years old for sex. Of course the girl was not harmed (and in fact, she was rescued and sent to a children's home), but the beginnings of what would otherwise have been a process of child sexual enslavement were publicised in the paper. Six Salvation Army members were arrested and charged with abduction, two of whom were sent to prison for brief periods. This audacious tactic caused huge public outcry and the Criminal Law Amendment Act raising the age of female sexual consent to sixteen was hurried through Parliament in 1885. What now seems to be common sense and basic morality had required courageous and creative action to come about.

Various creative actions and tactics have been already mentioned in this book: the Montgomery bus boycott, the AGM action by Abdul, the Nottingham Citizens' commission into hate crime, the cleaners leaving letters on ministers' desks; Ismael's action at Allianz with students in suits and CVs at the ready. They all involve some imaginative flair that tunes into the particular nature of the issue and the target, and increases the chances of getting noticed and getting a reaction. They are variations on the theme of collective public action. They require hard work and good organisational skills, but they do not require significant technology, finance or expertise beyond the reach of most people.

But what about different tactics: what about legal expertise and the power of the courts; what about the speed and reach of online campaigning and the huge audience and emotional pull of film? The rest of this chapter explores these tactics using inspirational examples and citing experts in those fields. To make the biggest impact, we need to build people power and develop sophisticated campaign strategies that combine the best of many different tactics, bringing together experts in those approaches at an early stage in campaign development.

I've been inspired by the work of ClientEarth, which has used strategic litigation to force the government to live up to its legal obligations on tackling air pollution. The CEO and founder, James Thornton, chose to focus on air pollution because winning a case on that issue could have a significant impact on public health, while also proving the potential of strategic litigation and increasing its use amongst environmental campaigners.

It was back in 2009 that ClientEarth first sent the British government a letter asking – politely – how it planned on meeting an existing legal obligation to reduce nitrogen dioxide gas (NO_2) pollution to safe levels by 2010. The issue is serious: an estimated

40,000 early deaths in the UK per year are linked to dangerously high NO_2 levels. However, it turned out that the government had no intention of meeting that legal obligation and thought it could get away with extending the deadline to 2025. ClientEarth took legal action against the government, and its team of lawyers have now won cases in the High Court, the Court of Appeal and the Supreme Court, with the government appealing and trying to avoid taking responsibility at every twist and turn.

The way that the power dynamics played out at the Supreme Court, by which point the publication of the plan to reduce NO_2 levels was already five years late, is remarkable. James Thornton describes what happened:

> So, the government stood up in the Supreme Court and said: 'We have no intention of complying with this law as soon as possible.' That's despite admitting that they had broken the law. They argued that there was no need to declare that they had breached the law, because they planned to write a new air quality plan at some point. We argued that the court should order the government to write a new plan and set them a clear timetable to do so. You can't have governments disobeying their own laws, otherwise we don't have democracy under the rule of law. Needless to say, the Supreme Court agreed with us, and ordered the government to comply – and in a rare move gave us permission to go straight back to court if that plan was rubbish. It was. And we did. And we won.

This shows the distinctive contribution of strategic litigation: that if you win, then the hard power of the law can force a very powerful and obstinate adversary to comply.

In April 2017, the government tried to use the upcoming general election as an excuse for not publishing its plans in the timescale required by the court, but now has finally done so – seven years after the levels of NO_2 were supposed to have been reduced. ClientEarth and others are contesting the substance of the plans and are pushing the government to go further. The campaign has been spearheaded by the legal challenge, though it included a lobbying and media campaign from the outset. In order to broaden the pressure, ClientEarth has been working to build a coalition of charities, schools and cyclist groups to add on-the-ground people power to its strategy for change. It's this combined, multipronged approach that is getting the results. James offers this advice to people setting up a campaign: 'Don't start with strategic litigation, but do start thinking about using the law. What would be great is if you could involve lawyers as you develop your campaign, to get their expertise from the beginning and spot the opportunities for strategic litigation.'

So, strategic litigation is a powerful tactic to force change once a legal obligation is in place, but it only works at that stage of a campaign. If the issue is still relatively unknown and is a long way from finding itself into law, then film and digital media can be powerful tools to reach huge numbers of people, and increase awareness and empathy through storytelling. The example that really moved me as a story and impressed me as a strategy for social change is the award-winning

Virunga by Grain Media and Violet Films. The documentary is about the Virunga National Park in the Congo and a small, besieged team of park rangers who are protecting this area of amazing beauty (it is a UNESCO World Heritage Site and the home of rare mountain gorillas) against the threat of local militias and the power of a multinational company interested in the park's oil. The film is beautiful and gripping and I strongly recommend you see it if you haven't already done so, simply because it's a great film. But also because of the way it moves the viewer to action. By the end of it, you've been drawn into this far-off world and a story of injustice and you are desperate to do something to help. And for once, there is something clear you can do that looks like it will make a difference. There is a call to action, a website and a campaign strategy about highlighting wrongdoing by oil company SOCO and its associates, and attempting to prevent its illegal activities within the park.

For decades, film-makers have been creating films with a social purpose to draw attention to an injustice and raise awareness amongst people and policy-makers. But as with the one-off mass protest that gets into the headlines but lacks a strategy for change, simply raising awareness through a documentary is unlikely to lead to impact. Joanna Natasegara, founder of Violet Films and award-winning producer of *Virunga* and *The White Helmets*, explains: 'Awareness is what a film does in the absence of anyone thinking about additional impact.' She describes the growing significance of 'impact-producing', where film is seen as a tool to achieve specific social-change objectives. It's the mirror of 'the action is

in the reaction' from earlier in this book, where you start
with the reactions you're looking to achieve and plan
and judge the action accordingly. The impact-producer
starts off with the objective and a theory of change,
and then designs a multi-strand campaign strategy to
achieve it, of which film is a part.

Joanna outlines three impact objectives that ran
through the strategy behind making *Virunga*. First, to
alert people to what's happening in the park. Second, to
stop the oil company from acting illegally in the park.
Third, to enable the opportunity for longer-term peace
and prosperity around the park. Clearly the reach of a
really successful film like *Virunga*, out on Netflix with
global subscriptions of 100 million, does raise awareness amongst a large audience. But this awareness is
not going to achieve objective two on its own. So the
team worked up a sophisticated campaign that included
corporate and shareholder engagement, plus strategic
litigation to go alongside the film and be boosted by
the attention the film was attracting. 'Film creates a
moment,' says Joanna, 'and you can plan to the release
timeline and hang a whole load of other tactics around
that, where you know that the film is going to bring it to
the forefront of people's minds.' They showed *Virunga*
in nine parliaments to galvanise influential politicians
as well as investors. And it worked. In 2014, SOCO
committed to end its activities in Virunga National
Park, and any other UNESCO World Heritage Sites.

Objective three is, of course, a longer game and the
team are still contributing to work on local economic
development, but again the particular legacy of the
film and its great influence is clear. It was a purposeful

decision to name the film after the park in order to make it harder for any oil company in the future to go there, because now everyone knows the name Virunga. Strikingly, Joanna's advice to people setting up a campaign is similar to James Thornton's about getting the range of experts around the table from the beginning: 'Reach out to the storytelling community, to film-makers and others, about your issue and your story. Don't try and make a film yourself; there are too many bad campaign films out there. Find people who are good at what they do and get them involved.'

Lastly, I want to look at the power of digital technology. As a case in point, if you've got thousands of people suddenly wanting to help because they've been moved by a film, then the best and maybe the only way to capture that spike in interest is through signing people up online and moving them to action at least initially through digital means. We experienced something similar in September 2015, when the shocking image of Aylan Kurdi, the Syrian toddler whose body was found washed up on a beach, was shared on social media and on newspaper front pages around the world. It was a moment that punched through the public consciousness in the most profound way, straight to the heart. It wasn't about news or politics any-more, but just about being human. I went on Al Jazeera news that evening about the UK government's response to the refugee crisis and just before going on, the make-up artist summed it up perfectly, saying: 'I never really thought about it [the war in Syria, the refugee crisis] before, until I saw that photo. I've got a three-year-old. That could have been my little boy.'

There was suddenly a huge appetite to do something, and working with digital campaigning groups Avaaz and 38 Degrees, within a few weeks, Citizens UK had tens of thousands of supporters up and down the country eager to help. David Babbs, executive director of 38 Degrees, describes the distinctive contribution of digital simply: 'It's about speed and scale.' Not just in the way that campaigners can respond to sudden jumps in interest from the public, but in the way that people can relate to politicians. 'Over the last fifty years, politics has sped up particularly because of the twenty-four-hour news cycle, and it means that decision-making is taking place ever more rapidly and in a media-political bubble,' he explains. '38 Degrees allows people power to catch up with that increased political cycle speed.'

This absolutely resonates because that bubble of conversation between politicians and journalists really drives the feeling that politics is a spectator sport rather than something that people can have a meaningful role in. One great example of impact is the 38 Degrees campaign in 2011 to stop the privatisation of UK woodlands, which involved 500,000 people signing their petition, 100,000 people emailing their MPs, and a crowdfunded poll that demonstrated wider public opposition. This rapid mobilisation of such large numbers scared the government off and plans to sell off the forests were scrapped. But David is also clear on the limitations: 'The days when techno-optimists were saying that the internet could solve our political problems are over. Social media has shown itself able to become nasty, self-referential and polarised. Also, there was a brief time at the beginning of our work when digital was so new that it had a shock impact on MPs. But now that's not the case. Petitions on their own don't tend to work.'

David sees the future for 38 Degrees like this: 'The main thing we are trying to do is innovate and find new ways to engage the people who've got involved first digitally and bring them together in real life.' More than that, it's the opportunity that digital has to connect to people who perhaps haven't been involved heavily in campaigns before, but that first easy step to click their support for an issue can be what brings them into deeper involvement. When you're trying to build real relationships between people who've first engaged online, there's an important place for the more relationship-oriented activity as well as the more political one. 'We're organising large-scale park clean-ups and picnics in the summer,' David continues, 'and that nice community activity is really about engaging large numbers of people so we're ready to fight to protect parks from any reductions in spending coming along the way.'

This was exactly the kind of approach Citizens UK used in the Refugee Welcome campaign, launched in the aftermath of the Aylan Kurdi photo. We worked from the large support base of tens of thousands of people who had first engaged online in that moment of public outcry, and then sifted through this support to develop real local engagement through a combination of more politically oriented campaigning and friendly community activity. Crucially, Citizens UK had been campaigning for about eighteen months before the child's photo hit the headlines and we had a campaign issue and strategy already worked out. We were campaigning for an increase in the number of Syrian refugees coming in through the Vulnerable Persons Resettlement Scheme (VPRS – which brings over mainly families from the conflict region) up to a target of 1,500 people from about 200 resettled so far: this was the more modest issue we had cut off from the massive problem, which we calculated might be winnable. But by the evening of the photo's publication, Citizens UK saw that the power analysis had shifted so dramatically that our new line was to be calling for 20,000 people resettled under the VPRS. We had an issue to work on and we also had a strategy that local campaigners could get involved in, which was persuading their local author-ities to sign up to the VPRS. This meant that there was a greater possible role for people than is sometimes the way with digital engagement, where you might only be able to subscribe to a newsletter or donate money.

From the tens of thousands of people who signed up to our campaign online we had to find those with drive and talent, the people who could really organise a local group and pressurise their local authority into taking refugees on the VPRS. Using initially a self-selection question online and then through phone conferences and one-to-one conversations, we found about seventy people who had the appetite to be local Refugees Welcome coordinators. In December 2015, we brought them together to receive training on how to build a team, power analyses, one-to-one conversations, and the balance between campaign and service. We knew that for many people their initial inclination wasn't to lobby their local councillor: they wanted instead to offer kindness to people who were suffering. So we included, alongside the strategy for power and politics, recommendations of how people could prepare practically to welcome refugees when they arrived.

Perhaps the most inspiring team that came out of this was the Refugee Welcome group in Bath, chaired by Bernie Howley. Bernie had never been involved in anything political before, but she had attended the training, volunteered to coordinate the Bath group and built a fantastic team. Knowing the time pressure, that every week that went by was another week that vulnerable families were stuck in refugee camps or compelled to make dangerous sea crossings, the group swiftly engaged Bath Council in the resettlement scheme and encouraged local communities to prepare a welcome. One primary school had its children write welcome cards ready to be given to newly arrived refugee families. In February 2016, a refugee family arrived with an eleven-month-old baby who needed urgent medical attention, which would never have been possible in the camps where the family had been stuck. The family were taken straight from the runway to the hospital and the baby survived, thanks to the efforts of Bernie and thousands of other people who had been moved to action by the tragic image of another child who was not fortunate enough to reach safety.

With a combination of local organising, digital technology, lobbying, film and media work, and a wide range of partners, the government did adopt the 20,000 target for Syrian refugees in the Vulnerable Persons Resettlement Scheme, and that coalition is now pushing for the inclusion of further vulnerable children and an extension of the scheme through to 2022.

Chapter 8
Finding the Time

Jumping ahead to read the end of a book is a bad habit – one we all do every now and then – and it's one of those temptations you tend to regret as you ruin the final twist in the plot. But in this case, I would completely understand and maybe even recommend it. In fact, I would be astonished if you've got to this point without thinking something like: 'That all sounds great but it's unrealistic. Yes, I'm angry and I want to change things, but how on earth would I have the time to do anything like that? Don't you know how busy I am?'

Well, I don't know how busy you are, but I know that as a country we have mostly got ourselves very busy. Between work, the commute, family and house-work, there is barely time to check your smartphone eighty-five times and fit in three hours of TV viewing per day (apparently those are the current UK averages). But my guess is that you don't watch anything like that amount of TV – and probably wouldn't want to even if you had the time. Because I believe you are genuinely busy with your job or studies, your friends and family, and your community.

Good. Because it's the busy people that we need. Those who are immersed in their work and their communities, who are driven to go the extra mile and to care for others; those are the people with the energy and relationships to change the world. And I know you're not happy with the way things are; I know you've got an itch to do more, or at least make more of an impact: that's why you're reading this book. So, how do you find the time amidst everything else? There's no point in having a cause and a method but no time to pursue it, so I'm going to give you seven ways to find the time. Some of this is a recap – and given we're coming towards the end, that's a good thing – and some of this is new, and mostly credited to others who've taught me.

LOOK AFTER YOURSELF

The first thing to avoid is trying to do everything and ending up burnt out and unable to do anything. People who are driven to make the world a better place tend to overlook the most important cause, which is to take care of their own health and well-being.

My friend Amol has a wonderful analogy that I'm sure he won't mind me borrowing. He describes his life as being like a gas cooker. In your teens and early twenties, you've got the 'friends and fun' hob on full, with 'work' (school, uni, first job) up a little bit as well to maybe gas mark 5. As you move into your mid- to late twenties, you start to turn up the 'work' hob to 6,

7, 8 as you're looking to make something of a career, and also the 'relationship' hob starts to go from 4, to 5, to 6. You want to keep the friends hob up high, and then, BANG! Maybe a parent gets ill, maybe you have your own baby. You realise the 'family' hob is down on 1, like almost going out and you suddenly need to turn it right up. The family hob goes up to 6 or 7, and something has to give. You turn the friends right down to 3, and through your thirties and forties you try and keep all four hobs – work, relationship, friends, family – as high as possible. But then suddenly, all four start to stutter – like the gas pressure is dodgy. And you realise you've been taking the most important one for granted. The oven. Yourself. Your own health. The one that all the other parts rely on. Don't burn out. I like that analogy. In my house I do nearly all the cooking (I'm no saint – I do very little of the cleaning) so I think about it a lot.

How do you relax? Reading a book, walking in the woods, or pints in the pub with mates. It's up to you – but everyone needs time for relaxation and rejuvenation. Tessa Jowell came to a Citizens UK training event and she said two really insightful things on this subject that have been helpful to me. First, that with people who are dedicated to service of one sort or another, one essential pre-condition of relaxing is giving yourself permission to relax. Spend some time reminding yourself of the good things that you are doing, so that when you do spend two hours for yourself, you are warm in the knowledge you deserve it. Second, 'in our public lives we are less indispensable than we think we are, but in our private lives we are more indispensable than we think we are'. A statement of practical wisdom born of experience. Someone else can chair that campaign meeting, but no one else can cover your child's school play. I'm not recommending you put social change above yourself or your loved ones. We don't need more sacrifice. We need more strategy.

WHAT DO YOU REALLY CARE ABOUT?

Most people who have made some kind of inspirational social change do so because they have a personal motivation. Something they experienced, something someone they love has suffered from, something they really needed. Yes, you might have the time to click on ten petitions a week – each one only taking a second – but if you're going to put sustained effort into changing something then it's worth really reflecting on what you care about. Your roots, your values, the people and causes most important to you.

Return to the stick person you drew of yourself and what's important to you. Spend some time with it. What is most meaningful to you? What would you want to be known for, to tell your children that you were part of, or made happen?

STOP DOING SOME THINGS AND DELEGATE OTHERS

The flip side to thinking about what's really important is realising what's not that important. What can you drop? Not to be morbid, but it's about recognising that one day we're going to die. Time is precious. And it's wasted on things that we do because we've always done them. We're creatures of habit – and we don't want to offend people – but that meeting that you've been going to for years, and it feels like a scene from *Groundhog Day*, but without Bill Murray being funny: just stop it.

Your democracy needs you to find time to work with dynamic people and exciting organisations that are creating change and a better future. Maybe it's time to stop watching the news and start making the news. Look through your diary to find things that fit this criteria:

a) You do them because you've done them for a long time.
b) They feel like tasks rather than opportunities.
c) They leave you with less energy rather than more.

Now, work through them with the kind of ruthlessness you need when you're clearing out clutter from the home. What would happen if I just quit this? Would anything bad happen? Remember, you're less indispensable than you think you are.

If simply quitting is not possible, then delegate. If this has become routine for me, who else is it an opportunity for? Investing two hours finding someone who will take on that weekly responsibility you've been carrying for ages will save you forty hours over the year once they take it off your plate. One of the things that gets in the way of delegation is feeling too busy. We don't feel we have the time to find someone else who might do it and support them to do so. But that's a vicious circle. The more pressure we feel, the less we are able to involve others, the more there is for us to do.

One simple antidote is changing your to-do list. Make two columns: one with what the task is, and the second column with who else could do it with some encouragement. Then before starting to work through your list, spend fifteen minutes running through each task to see if someone else can do it instead.

WEAVE SOCIAL CHANGE INTO YOUR LIFE

We have power through relationships with other people. So the greatest possibility for social change starts with the people we know and can most easily connect to – in our neighbourhoods, our community organisations, affiliations and workplaces. The greatest potential for change also comes with the greatest convenience, because we already spend time with those people and those organisations. We don't have to start a whole new life of activity. It is all about mapping those networks you're in and working out where the potential is for power and change. Unlocking the possibilities through one-to-one conversations, listening, and looking for leaders. It's not the one-off event, and it doesn't require a superhuman ability or saintly disposition. It just means getting stuck in on a day-to-day basis in a sustainable way.

DO IT AS PART OF A TEAM

Life happens when you least expect it.

Your phone is stolen and you desperately need to replace it, worried you've lost your calendar, let alone your photos (yes, this happened to me during the writing of this book, and the big lesson: don't ignore repeated messages saying that your cloud is deactivated). Your child has been bitten on the face by another child at nursery, and you need to cancel meetings and pick him up early (also happened). You spill water over your laptop on the final weekend of writing and have to get your stepbrother to pull the back off with pliers to access the hard drive and save the files (you couldn't make it up). When that stuff happens, we need to be able to rely on others. It's not possible to do things alone.

Time spent investing in your team is time well spent, because they'll have your back and provide cover when the time comes. Making change happen often takes years and it might be that you step back and others take it on from you. So being part of a team and an organisation means the work can live on beyond the time you can give to it.

BE STRATEGIC AND MAKE A PLAN

Big companies are often good at strategy. They spend millions of pounds on training, research and development. They've got two-year strategies, five-year strategies, twenty-year strategies. These companies have a plan for you. What you will buy. What you will see online. What your town and city will be like in a decade.

But what do communities spend on training and development? How many churches or schools or neighbourhood associations have a ten-year strategy for their own organisation, let alone for influencing the wider world? Have you and your neighbours got a neighbourhood plan? Do you have a plan for yourself? Because other people have got a plan for you.

TAKE CONTROL OF YOUR SCHEDULE — AND HAVE ONE-TO-ONE CONVERSATIONS

If we don't fill our diaries, someone else will, so get your calendar out/up on the screen. Those days and weeks and months: that's your life, that's the one chance you have to be who you want to be and make a difference. So, take control of the schedule, take yourself seriously (not too seriously) and think what you really need and want for yourself, for others and for society.

For some people, creating social change is something that is part of their work, or can be integrated into it. But even if that's not the case there is time. Every week has 168 hours and here's how it could break down:

1 Sleep – 49 hours
2 Recreation and family and friends – 40 hours
3 Work and travel – 50 hours
4 Tasks and housework – 15 hours

That leaves 14 hours per week to dedicate to the cause you believe in and the issue you're angry about. To spend on one-to-one conversations and taking action for social change. And that would change the world.

Chapter 9
The Iron Rule

There's one more principle in the method of community organising that needs to be covered, and for me it's the most challenging – but also the most radical and profound. There's no escaping it. It's even called 'the Iron Rule'.

Never do for others what they can do for themselves.

It exposes the earnest do-gooder who always knows what's best for others, and it pours scorn on the armchair liberal worrying about the plight of the poor. It pushes us towards justice rather than charity, towards organising rather than service delivery, and towards a relentless focus on the development of leadership and democratic skills amongst the people. It means that if we want to do some good in the world, we must build the power of people.

It's also hard to follow and uncomfortable to apply. It might be the Iron Rule, but I find myself breaking it every day. Often it's because I'm in a rush and it's quicker (in the short term) to do things myself rather than wait or help others to do it for themselves. Sometimes I underestimate the ability of people and think I have to do it when in fact they were perfectly capable, and, if I'm honest, sometimes I want to be the hero. But whatever the reason, breaking the Iron Rule just makes me too busy, and it also stops others growing and taking responsibility. Trying to live up to the Iron Rule prompts a constant argument about what people are able to do and what they're not, and it pushes us towards a stronger belief in the capacity of people and a deeper trust in their motives.

Along with most of what Saul Alinsky said and did, the Iron Rule is designed to provoke creative tension and a reaction. It provides a powerful counterbalance to the fact that people with less money and power so often feel like they are constantly being 'done to', that decisions about their lives and communities are taken elsewhere, even by those who say they are trying to help. This disempowerment feeds feelings of distrust, apathy and blame, the conditions needed for a divisive populism to spread. The Iron Rule, by contrast, requires us to make people the authors of the change they want, which then breeds confidence, agency and collaboration between people. It reinforces the argument for an invigoration of our political culture, towards a new populism of the people by the people. The implications of the Iron Rule are radical and far-reaching, for individuals who want to make the world a better place, for the need to move from charity to justice, and for organisations that aim to help people.

On a personal level, and bringing it right back to the everyday, my two-year-old is just about to start potty training. Now, I have a choice: either I can keep changing the nappies, which I admit I don't particularly like but I've got pretty quick at, or I can take the plunge and remove the nappies. Is he ready? I don't know. Am I going to get poo on my carpet? Yes. It might take a while and it might be messy, but unless I stop doing things for him that he can do for himself, I might still be changing his nappies when he's twenty-five, and that's not good for anybody.

Individuals who want to make the world a better place are constantly doing things for other people. That's good – if those are things that those people genuinely want and can't do for themselves. But not if it's something that others could be doing. Otherwise we think we're helping – but actually we're just prolonging their dependency on us, stopping them learning and making us stressed and busy. The Iron Rule means delegating, letting go, challenging people to do things themselves and, crucially, focusing our efforts on building other people's capacity and leadership.

The stories I've told in this book are in some ways misleading. I've been guilty of the same simplification that I called out in the introduction, that in telling social change stories we tend to place a single named hero or heroine at the heart, rather than the real story of a collective effort. The success of Rosa Parks, Abdul Durrant, Ismael Musoke, Katy Rojas, Bernie Howley and so on wasn't in their individual excellence, but in the way that they brought others together and agitated and supported them to take action. For those of us who want to build people power for change, it becomes more and more about how we can develop the capacity of other people and less about a symbolic statement of our own values. The one-off mobilisations don't allow for people to learn and grow, whereas working together on incremental changes enables the focus to shift towards developing the skills and leadership of ourselves and others through the campaign.

The Iron Rule also has big implications for the kind of change we are aiming for and who sets the agenda. It means we must have the people who are experiencing the problem first-hand at the centre of determining the solution. In my experience, that's where the simplest and most radical ideas are born. In the early days of the Living Wage campaign we had a slogan: 'Justice, not charity'. The reason for that was threefold. First, when the cleaners on poverty wages said what they wanted, it wasn't handouts. It was to be paid enough to live and for dignity in their working lives. Second, it was a message to the big banks in Canary Wharf who, when we demanded that they pay the Living Wage, would respond by pointing us to their glossy corporate social responsibility portfolios: bankers out on team-building days painting school walls and planting trees; donating to local charities, and so on. Charity was used as an excuse not to take responsibility for the injustice of thousands of people working days and nights to keep their offices clean and their employees fed, but not paid enough to provide for their families.

Finally, it was a message to the communities themselves. The churches ran soup kitchens and the schools ran breakfast clubs. And when they paused the giving-out of food for a moment and asked the question why people were there, the response was not that people were lazy, or that there was no work to find. Many of them were working, but it wasn't enough to pay the bills. Working full-time and having to choose between heating and eating. It's a situation that calls for a structural change rather than just a sticking plaster. I think about low-paid cleaners I've met who were managing the most unbelievable schedules: multiple shifts, kids and long bus journeys because they couldn't afford the tube. Their diaries were just as difficult as the chief exec's and there was no PA to help. And then they were fined if they were late to work by ten minutes. People deserve more than charity. They deserve power and justice. The Iron Rule demands that we stop just helping people and start working with them to achieve what they really want.

'When I give food to the poor, they call me a saint. When I ask why the poor have no food, they call me a communist.'

ARCHBISHOP CÂMARA

That simple and powerful question 'Why?' made all the difference one cold autumn morning in the 'jungle' camp of Calais. A small team of four from Citizens UK had gone out to Calais to explore opportunities for action and change. As the team wandered about, they saw groups of refugees gathered by nationality and language – the Eritreans, Syrians, the Afghanis, the Egyptians, and so on. The smells from the fires, mostly of burning plastic, mixed with the raw sewage dribbling down the streets. Rubbish and makeshift tarpaulin tents were everywhere and it was clear that here were several thousand people in desperate circumstances. This dangerous and desolate feeling of a refugee camp was strangely mixed up with the appearance of an alternative festival, because dotted around there were scores of volunteers wearing wellington boots and doing things like setting up camp theatres and soup kitchens. The heightened public awareness and sympathy had brought loads of people to the camp to help, and also flooded it with donations – often the wrong sort, such as bottled water for a camp where this was one of the only things already provided and baby clothes for a community with many children but very few under the age of ten.

The team headed for the area where the Syrian refugees were gathered, knowing that it was this community for whom there was the greatest opportunity for a political resolution of their situation, given the heightened levels of public support for Syrians following the photo of Aylan Kurdi and the media coverage of the war. They found a group of elders who then brought others together – a group of about forty, including many teenagers. After some initial introductions the team asked the Syrians: 'Why are you here, stuck waiting in this camp, when Germany is open?'

'We want to go to the UK.'

'Why?'

There were several answers to that question: jobs, language, safety. But there was one answer that opened up an opportunity for change.

'Because my uncle is there,' said one teenage boy.

And that simple answer was the beginning of the Citizens UK Safe Passage project – because it raised the possibility not just of immediate assistance to people in a desperate situation, but of actually solving the problem they were facing. The potential lay in an underused bit of legislation that could see these children reunited with their families safely and legally. The Dublin regulation requires asylum seekers to claim asylum in the first safe country they arrive in, and in Europe that often means Italy or Greece. The UK deports about 1,000 people per year back to the frontiers of Europe through these provisions. The same regulation, though, says that where a child has a family member in another EU state, they should be able to request transfer to join them. But these provisions for family reunion had never once worked from France to Britain and there were hundreds of children in that position with family members in the UK. With the system failing, teenagers were dying on the tracks of the Eurostar and under the wheels of lorries, trying to reach their loved ones. They weren't about to give up, because they had travelled thousands of dangerous miles; many of them had either lost parents and siblings to the war or had left them behind, because there was something they wanted – to be with family and to be safe. And it was by asking the direct question and getting down to that real self-interest, rather than assuming we knew what they needed, that we reached a proposition for justice and a possibility for real change.

Within a couple of weeks, the team was back in the camps with pro bono lawyers to start to process claims. It was a race against time, because each night these young people, who had a moral and legal case to enter Britain safely, were risking their lives. The first child to lose his life while the legal work was under-way, and whose case was part of our legal challenge to the government, was fifteen-year-old Afghan, Masud. He suffocated in a lorry as he attempted to reach the UK and join his family here. The following month we won the first test case and four Syrian boys stuck in the Calais 'jungle' travelled legally and safely to be reunited with their families in Britain. Since then, working with allies including Lord Alf Dubs, who was himself a child refugee saved from Nazi Germany, we have seen a further 1,100 vulnerable children travel through the routes we have opened.

The Iron Rule doesn't say 'don't do things for people', and it's good that people are moved to give time and money when people genuinely need it. But the Iron Rule means we can't stop with charity. We have to ask the 'why' questions; we have to take seriously the answers and be prepared for that to lead us into ques-tions of power and politics. Take food banks.

The Trussell Trust runs the primary network of food banks in the UK. In 2015–16, they had an esti-mated 40,000 volunteers working across 424 food banks giving out a total of 1.1 million food parcels. (The Trussell Trust represents only about a third of the total number of emergency food-assistance projects, so you might treble these numbers.) The trust asks people why they have no food, and the reasons cited by people coming to food banks are:

1. Benefit delays or benefits changes (40 per cent)
2. Low income (23 per cent)
3. Debt (7 per cent)
4. Unemployment (5 per cent)

So what does this tell us? We need to improve the benefits system and we need decent jobs – otherwise it's just more and more food banks. It's not dignified: people rely on the handouts of others when often they are working but just paid a pittance and work irregular hours – or they have been caught up in a benefits delay and are without income for weeks on end. Yes, if people are suffering then it's good to try and help: share food, donate money and give time. It's a start. But if that's where we stop, then we are complicit. In fact, there is a great opportunity for power and justice stored up in all the effort and goodwill that goes into charitable service. There are tens of thousands of people who volunteer at food banks up and down the country. Let's say that you're one of them. You've read this book and have decided to take up the radical challenge of the Iron Rule and start using the method for change outlined here to try and tackle some of underlying causes bringing people to food banks. What would you do? Let's recap:

1. Map out a power analysis of the food bank and start having one-to-one conversations

with core volunteers and organisers in order
to establish trust and influence in the project;
find allies who are also angry at the underlying causes and want to do something about it.

2 Start having one-to-ones with people who
use the food bank and ask respectfully why
they come. Look for people with the anger
and interest to fight for change, and an
experience of injustice that could galvanise
a campaign. Perhaps a family forced to the
breadline because they made a mistake on
a form and have had their benefits stopped
for a month? Or a worker who's stuck on an
unpredictable zero-hours contract and works
for a profitable and reputable employer?

3 Working together as a team, you start to
build a campaign, following the Research,
Action, Evaluation steps outlined in Chapter
6: starting with a listening campaign, a power
analysis and moving from problem to issue. It
turns out that a prominent high-street retailer
is using and abusing zero-hours contracts and
you pick this as the target, aiming to have
them agree to offer permanent contracts and
regular hours to everyone who's been there for
more than six months.

4 You take an action: maybe you set up a
temporary food bank outside the store to
make it easier for people who need to supple-
ment their earned income with donated food,
with all the attention that brings to the shop's
reputation.

5 The action provokes a reaction and over
the next year, through further action and
negotiation, the store agrees to implement
a more responsible approach to zero-hours
and permanent contracts. The volunteers and
people using the food bank grow in confidence, skills and power and start to look to
bigger issues.

In that simple question 'Why?' lies the potential shift from charity to justice. And through the
Iron Rule, the focus along the whole journey of the
campaign is about building the capacity of people,
with the people who use the food bank and volunteer
at the food bank working together to tackle the causes
of food poverty. Who knows, maybe that campaign
would be the beginning of a coalition of hundreds
of food banks and local organisations that campaign
together to end punitive benefits sanctions – or make
some other massive difference.

Finally, the Iron Rule has radical implications for
organisations that set out in one way or another to
help people. Even more than well-meaning individuals, these organisations have a tendency to break
the Iron Rule. The hierarchy, the bureaucracy, the
role of the expert professional, all that combines to
squeeze out the potential of the people themselves,
who become passive clients and customers rather
than active citizens responsible for tackling problems
collectively. The same costs that apply to individuals
who break the Iron Rule apply to organisations, but
magnified, because the more the organisation treats

people as passive recipients of a service, the more they come to need the help of an increasingly busy set of staff. You see it in different ways in the health service, in charities, in trade unions, in churches, and so on. Of course there's a vast amount that experts in those organisations provide that people can't do themselves. I wouldn't want to be asked to perform my own open-heart surgery. But if health is just about helping patients once they get ill rather than enabling people to get together and tackle the causes of ill health, then there's never going to be enough money to keep it going. If the trade union sells itself as an insurance policy then there's never going to be enough paid staff to solve everyone's problem, let alone any real collective power in the workplace. If schools are just factories for test results, then where are children going to learn that their voice matters, that democracy means they have the power and the responsibility to shape the future, and develop the skills to do so?

So what does it mean in practical terms for an organisation to grapple with the Iron Rule and to shift from delivering a service to individuals, to building capacity for collective action? Let's take the way schools relate to parents and see the difference.

I was asked by a headteacher who complained that parents were not engaging enough in their children's education to help him connect to parents. The school had recently employed a 'parent engagement manager' who had initiated fortnightly coffee mornings for parents. As well as the posters he had put up around the school and the letters sent home, I recommended he have brief face-to-face conversations at the school gates to invite parents personally. When eighteen parents came to the first coffee morning it was a good start. We worked out that fifteen of them were parents he had personally invited, three came because of the letter home and none because of the posters.

The meeting began with the parents, the parent engagement manager, the headteacher and me all sitting around having tea and biscuits. As ever, we started with a round of introductions to understand a bit more about self-interest: what's your name; what year are your children in; what concerns or ideas do you have about the school or neighbourhood? We started to go round.

'My name is Anne, with a daughter in Year Eight, and I'm worried about the behaviour of children…'

And before she could finish, the head interrupted.

'Oh no, you don't have to worry about that – we have a new behaviour strategy that we are implementing.'

And the second parent.

'My name is Amin, I have a girl in Year Ten, and I have heard that the road outside the school is very unsafe and I'm worried that there's going to be an accident.' A few other parents nodded their heads or murmured agreement.

And again, the head came in with: 'Yes, we're aware of that and I will write to the council today – don't worry, we've got that in hand.'

This is the service-delivery culture in action: the experts are in charge and it leaves no space for people to get involved.

So what happens when you inject the Iron Rule and the community organising method?

Here's another parents' coffee morning, this time at a different school, Randal Cremer Primary in Hackney. The opening question is the same: introduce yourself and say what concerns you.

'My name is Katie and I'm worried because there's damp in our flat and the children aren't sleeping well. They're coughing all night.'

This time the family support worker, Edward Ablorh, who has been on community organising training, responds: 'That sounds difficult – have you tried to do something about that?'

Katie: 'Well I've called Hackney Homes loads of times, but they didn't respond. I tried to complain, but they say it's our fault with the cooking and steam.'

There are murmurs of agreement in the room and someone speaks out, saying how their child's just been diagnosed with bronchitis and the doctor is concerned about the damp.

So Edward says: 'Sounds like that's a real concern and other people feel the same. Katie, would you be able to bring together five people who have that same issue? And who else here cares about that too? Would you be able to bring some people along to a meeting? Let's do something about it.'

From that first coffee morning, Katie started to stand out. She had never played a public role, she had no position in the school or anywhere else and she would never have thought of herself as political. But when she spoke, the other parents listened.

Towards the end of the meeting, a couple of sceptical parents voiced their doubts: 'There's no point in bothering. We've all tried to get them to come and sort out the damp but they won't.'

It was when Katie said, 'It's surely worth another go,' that the group agreed to move forward with a campaign.

They started knocking on doors and asking people two questions. First, are you experiencing problems with damp in your home? Second, do you want to join a campaign to do something about it? The stories of damp and mould were shocking. Parents with eczema, kids missing school with respiratory problems and toadstools growing in bedrooms. But maybe the answers to the second question were worse. People had lost hope that anything would change. They said things like: 'They'll never listen. There's nothing we can do. They say it's our fault because of the cooking and that we should open the windows, but then we're worried the children will be cold.' It's what always happens, people turn their powerlessness inwards and they blame themselves, when in fact, it's a housing crisis and a landlord that won't take responsibility. It gets me angry and it's happening all the time. The organising culture aims to turn that individual despair and frustration into collective anger and power for change.

So, six weeks after the initial coffee morning there's now a team of parents from Randal Cremer and from other local schools and communities working together as part of Shoreditch Citizens, and they're holding an event to decide on campaign priorities. Katie and the team have brought along about fifty parents who have been involved in the campaign so far, and she is standing up on the stage, with the headteacher to her side, ready to speak for the first time in public. Charlotte Graves, the chief executive of Hackney Homes, has turned down the invitation to meet the parents and hear their concerns. Up on stage Katie's response is: 'If she won't come to us, then we'll have to go to her.'

The following week about a hundred people from Shoreditch Citizens, led by Katie and the team, go down to the Hackney Homes head office. They set up their own mock complaints desk right on the steps and start logging about seventy individual concerns into one big complaints list. The local newspaper is present taking photos when the list is delivered to Hackney Homes. By the end of that day a date is agreed for a meeting with Charlotte Graves and within the year they have won over £1.2 million of fast-tracked remedial work for damp across ten residential blocks. Hackney Homes initiates a new training programme for their surveyors to improve the way they recognise the structural causes of damp, as opposed to laying the blame on residents' behaviour. The children sleep better at night and suffer fewer health problems growing up in homes that aren't damp. And Katie and the other parents can tell their children, with utter conviction, that you can make a difference if you try.

The Iron Rule requires us to see people differently. Not as problems or burdens, clients or customers, but as citizens who can make a difference for themselves and others. It means shifting from always trying to solve people's problems, or ignoring the underlying causes of them, to building the capacity of people for collective action and political change. We are faced with a market culture that is spending hundreds of millions of pounds on advertising, telling us that our primary role in life is to be a consumer, and with a dominant political culture telling us that we are spectators in a game played out in Westminster and in TV studios. In standing up to this and providing an alternative vision, we all have a role to play. Local organisations must be brave, and realise their democratic purpose in helping people learn how to find their voice, and develop the skills and attitudes to be citizens. And each of us as individuals, in whatever way, big or small, must connect with our sense of injustice and channel that anger into effective action.

What ties the stories told in this book together is not the severity of the problems faced or the scale of the impacts made. It is who the protagonists are. These are not stories of elected politicians, policy experts or benevolent business people deciding what is best for others, but of people themselves working out what they want and coming together to achieve it.

So, what's the story they will write about you?

Acknowledgements

I would like to recognise some of the people without whom this book, and more importantly the method and the justice described within it, would not have happened.

Neil Jameson, who founded community organising in the UK, and a visionary, a fighter and a dear friend. He had the determination to create something from nothing in the face of scepticism and despite initial failure. He is instinctively on the side of the oppressed and is instinctively strategic at the same time – a special combination.

The cleaners and low-paid workers who led the hard end of the Living Wage campaign – Abdul, Emmanuel, June, Juliana, Benedita, Katy, Martha, Julieta, Valdemar, the Sanchez family, to name a few. They risked so much more than I did. Their bravery has won a Living Wage for hundreds of thousands of others.

The Industrial Areas Foundation, which developed the curriculum that we use. What a great gift to have a method that works.

Bernadette Farrell, who taught us all that songs and gifts are more powerful than placards and criticism. Kaneez Shaid – a constant inspiration to me over the last decade. The talented and courageous team of colleagues, leaders, trustees, funders and supporters who make Citizens UK happen.

Joanna Natasegara, Orlando Von Einsiedel, David Babbs and James Thornton for their inspirational work and their time in contributing to this book.

Alexis Kirschbaum for the idea, the enthusiasm and clear feedback when needed. And everyone who helped me in the writing: Amol, Charlie, Charlotte, Dan, Frances, George, James, John, Jonathan, Leah, Lizzie, Mubin, Owen, Stefan and Tess.

My mum and my dad – for everything.

A Note on the Author

MATTHEW BOLTON, Deputy Director of Citizens UK and Lead Organiser for London Citizens, has built a nationwide alliance of thousands of community campaigners who together have driven forward two of the most effective, strategic and widest-reaching campaigns in the UK of the past two decades – and he's only thirty-five. He led the UK Living Wage campaign, which has now won over £200 million for 150,000 low-paid workers and has persuaded the Government to introduce the 'National Living Wage', benefitting millions more. The Refugee Welcome and Safe Passage campaign have secured entry for over 2,000 vulnerable Syrian children, including hundreds from the 'jungle' camps of Calais. Matthew coaches community organisers across the country, and is a Trustee of the London Community Land Trust affordable housing provider. He lives with his wife and young son in South London.

A Note on the Type

A Note on the Type

The text of this book is set Adobe Garamond. It is one of several versions of Garamond based on the designs of Claude Garamond. It is thought that Garamond based his font on Bembo, cut in 1495 by Francesco Griffo in collaboration with the Italian printer Aldus Manutius. Garamond types were first used in books printed in Paris around 1532. Many of the present-day versions of this type are based on the *Typi Academiae* of Jean Jannon cut in Sedan in 1615.

Claude Garamond was born in Paris in 1480. He learned how to cut type from his father and by the age of fifteen he was able to fashion steel punches the size of a pica with great precision. At the age of sixty he was commissioned by King Francis I to design a Greek alphabet, and for this he was given the honourable title of royal type founder. He died in 1561.